THE TYPICAL TEXAN

"The fistfight the cowpunchers, the fire.

"The forthright, the courageous, the free."

THE
TYPICAL
TEXAN

Biography of an American Myth

JOSEPH LEACH

SOUTHERN METHODIST UNIVERSITY PRESS
DALLAS : 1952

Library of Congress Catalog Card Number 52-11833

PRINTED IN THE UNITED STATES OF AMERICA
AT EL PASO, TEXAS

To the memory of

LEANDER HOSEA LEACH

in whose pioneer veins
my blood came west
to Texas

ACKNOWLEDGMENTS

MY DEBTS for help on this book were not all incurred in the actual process of research and writing. In many cases the assistance was of an extremely indirect nature. Vague suggestions and casual expressions of interest in the subject often proved later on to be of great benefit, and I have realized only recently that some of the most valuable favors done me were the ones of which I was least aware at the time.

I know now that my preparation for this book actually began long before I could spell Texas, when my grandfathers used to tell my brother Austin and me about the experiences of their boyhood in Texas, in the days when their families' only neighbors were other pioneers—and Indians. I wish especially that my paternal grandfather could have read this book, because I know now that it was he who first made me want to write it. I like to think that he would have enjoyed what I have written on a subject dear to his heart, even though it deals somewhat more dispassionately with Indians than he ever deigned to do.

Many other people have contributed just as indirectly to these pages. Though I am all too aware that any "credit" list will unavoidably remain incomplete, I should like to express my sincere thanks to the following people for kindnesses which they have probably forgotten: Miss Ethel Morgan of Wichita Falls, a great teacher who in the sixth grade opened my eyes and my imagination to Texas history as well as to a host of other good, unforgettable things; Dr. Madge Davis of Midwestern University for encouragement and inspiration far beyond the call of her professorial duties; Professor John McGinnis of Southern Methodist University, who, even more than his beloved Shakespeare, held the mirror up to life for me and proved it good; Professors E. E. Leisy and John Lee Brooks of the same university, for many favors done me while I was their student and after; J. Frank Dobie, who wished me "good hunting" one morning on Waller Creek; Professor Edward Everett Dale of the University of Oklahoma; Dr. B. A. Botkin for helping me, with all the force of his knowledge and character, to launch and complete this study; Professor Richard Dorson of Michigan State College; my major professors at Yale University, Stanley Williams and Ralph H. Gabriel, the latter of whom supervised much of the research behind this book, which began its life (in more academic form) as a doctoral dissertation; James Howard; Miss Nelle Smither; W. A. Philpott of Dallas; the many officials of the rare book collections at Yale, the Library of Congress, the University of Texas, and the New York Public Library, without whose kindness I could never have used the priceless materials which figure in this book. In particular I am indebted to Mrs. Marcelle Hamer and Miss Kathleen Blow of the University of Texas Library. I acknowledge a deep sense of gratitude to my colleagues at Texas Western College, especially the following, who have advised me and have proofread parts or all of the ensuing pages: C. L. Sonnichsen, Haldeen Braddy, and Francis Fugate.

I have been extremely fortunate in the editorial guidance I have received while preparing this book. To Mrs. Margaret L. Hartley of Southern Methodist University Press I extend my sincere thanks.

For permission to quote from his poem, "America Was Promises," I am indebted to Archibald MacLeish, and to Alfred A. Knopf, Inc., for permission to quote from D. W. Brogan's book, *The American Character*.

A portion of this work, in slightly different form, appeared in the *Southwest Review* (Spring, 1950) as "Crockett's Almanacs and the Typical Texan." I wish to thank the editor of that magazine for permission to reprint the material here.

Only one person have I consciously plagiarized—my wife, Dorothy, many of whose questions gave rise to ideas in this book. Without her very real participation in this project from the start, it would have been impossible for me to bring it to a close.

JOSEPH LEACH

El Paso del Norte
May 21, 1952

CONTENTS

CONTENTS

ILLUSTRATIONS

Frontispiece by José Cisneros

They Call Him Tex

About 1886, a Fort Worth newspaper gave space to a rambunctious fellow who seemed badly in need of telling the world about himself. Most of the world had never heard of the *Fort Worth Daily Gazette,* but almost everybody had heard, years before, of Texans like "The Wild Cowhand."

> I'm a buzzard from the Brazos on a tear
> Hear me hoot.
> I'm a litter of the flowing locks of hair
> Watch 'em scoot.
> I'm a coyote of the sunset, prairie dude
> Hear me zip.
> In the company of gentlemen I am rude
> With my lip.
>
> Those who love me call me Little Dynamite
> I'm a pet.
> I'm a walking, stalking terror of the night
> You can bet.
> With my nickel plated teaser
> Many a rusty featured greaser's
> Sun has set.
>
> Sometimes I strike an unprotected town
> Paint it red.
> Choke the sheriff, turn the marshal upside down
> On his head.
> Call for drinks for all the party
> And if chinned by any smarty
> Pay in lead.[1]

By 1860 the Typical Texan was pretty well crystallized along the line of "The Wild Cowhand" and fellows like him. He was not the only American type who was taken to represent a whole section of the country, but he filled one of the brighter spots in the limelight. Big of wind and limb, he stood out in any company and always made himself heard.

One of the better and more popular humorists of the post-Civil War years, Alexander Sweet, was himself a Texan. He knew from experience what non-Texans thought about natives of his home state. Sweet came to realize in New York that wherever he went people compared him in the flesh to an abstract notion they expected him, as a Texan, to match. In 1882 the humorist described this much-admired and much maligned character.

"The Typical Texan," Sweet wrote, "is a large-sized Jabberwock, a hairy kind of gorilla, who is supposed to reside on a horse. He is half-alligator, half-human, who eats raw buffalo, and sleeps out on the prairie." For protection he carries four or five revolvers at his belt, and a large assortment of cutlery in his boot. To fail to invite him to a drink is more dangerous than kicking a can of dynamite, for at best, the Typical Texan is peaceable only after he has killed everybody in sight and can find no fresh material to practice on.[2]

The Typical Texan talked as lustily as he fought. Anything that impressed him, impressed him mightily. His talk of it reverberated to the skies. He boasted about his superior physical capacities: "Show me the honery crittur thinks he can lick me in a fight!" He waxed eloquent about Texas, "the garden spot of the world and God's own special country." Or when temporarily soured on the place, he still found Texas the most wonderfully "cussed" spot in creation, and he talked like the half-starved fellow who stuck his head out the window when a judge was passing his farm and said, "Judge, I ain't so poor as you think me to be, for I don't own this 'ere land."[3] In the company of women, chivalry motivated his every action. A man of "innate nobility and high-toned sense of honor" was the way one lady described him in 1858.[4]

The legendary Texan is a lineal descendant of older American character types, but no one has ever argued that he was wholly the product of heredity. He was, in reality, a product of many elements. Art combined with fact to form him. Just as movies, fiction, radio, and television now help to keep him alive, there were similarly effective agents before Appomattox which joined forces to aid in his creation.

The Typical Texan was bred of a union of suggestions on the stage, in the stories and novels, almanacs, newspapers, magazines, and travel books of the nineteenth century, but such treatments really deserve only part of the credit. He was not wholly the son of vivid imaginations. He was partly the son of truth. Factual descriptions of actual Texans aided in establishing the high-flown notion. Historical figures such as Sam Houston and Big-Foot Wallace, as well as myriads of lesser lights, figured in its formation. The unknown Texas citizens who fascinated visitors were responsible, too, for many of the impressions which such travelers broadcast in print when they returned home. Probably no person ever lived who was "the spit and image" of the mythical "Texian," as Lone Star men once called themselves. But many men resembled him closely, and others valiantly tried to measure up to him.

Today, the "Texian" is well over a hundred years old, yet he carries his age well. His friends of the 1840's would say he hasn't changed a bit. Present-day Texans grow up aware that a special aura surrounds them when they step outside their native state. Though at home their personal brush with this "Texan Tradition" may have been only at the movies and in the comic books, whenever they leave home they confront the fabled portrait of Texans which outsiders have kept dusted off for at least four generations. If they realize what is coming they sometimes buy white Stetsons, ram their feet into stiff new cowboy boots, and try to remember the last time they rode a horse or saw an Indian. All this they do in the interest of keeping the picture bright.

At the mid-point of the twentieth century people the world over know of the Typical Texan. In 1947 a Japanese at Kokura, who had never forgotten the impression William S. Hart movies made on him in the 1920's, acknowledged my introduction as a Texan by asking, "*Anata* [you], cowboy?" Similarly, though the "cowboy" knew nothing about New Zealanders, some men from Down Under whom he once met felt they knew what he was

like: they exclaimed knowingly, "Ho-ho! a Texan, eh!" Recently,
when a member of the British embassy staff in Washington announced her plans to visit Texas, the ambassador, the late Lord
Inverchapel, commending her adventurous spirit, exclaimed,
"How *sporting* of you!" Another Britisher, who spent an evening
not long ago with some Texas friends, outlasted the occasion—
though the next morning found him praying for early death and
bigger aspirins. Since then, according to the *El Paso Herald-
Post,* he goes around London, thumping his chest and pro-
claiming to everyone, "Ah, but I've survived a Texan's 'quiet
evening.' "5

The Texan reputation is, of course, much better known to
Americans. In the nation's capital, where the westerner (since
David Crockett's famous years in Congress) has had a peculiar
notoriety, I asked why a certain towering West Virginian was
called "Tex." His friend told me, "Because he looks like a
Texan." In Connecticut nobody took me for one, because even
in boot heels I am barely five-ten. All Texans in the armed forces
during World War II were constantly aware that their fellows
expected them to cavort "like Texans," which meant simply that
they should act and talk big about Texas and everything that
concerned it.

The common notion of Texas is now so deeply rooted that
few people have any idea where and how it originated. Most of
them think simply "what everybody has always thought about
Texans." To them, Texans are big fellows, ready to fight at the
drop of a hint (or the fluttering of a lady's comely eyelid), and
bursting with brag about Texas. "Texans can all ride like Hopalong Cassidy, shoot like Buffalo Bill, and orate about Texas like
the Senate's white-maned Tom Connally." Outsiders also think
most of the Texans are oil barons, cattle barons, cotton barons,
and barons of other kinds who can make money like Croesus;
but this is a mere detail in the over-all figure that the Typical
Texan cuts nationally.

Today, "Tex" is unique. Neither the Californian nor the
Brooklynite, each of whom is able enough when it comes to
venting local spirit, possesses a reputation quite as colorful as

that of the Texan. Though no Californian or trans-East River New Yorker ever underplayed the virtues of his native community, neither type is traditionally recognizable on sight, as Texans are thought to be. All three are expected to possess an ebullient state of mind that habitually leavens their talk; this is superlatively true of the Typical Texan. In addition, "Tex" is notable for a characteristic physique. And he is chivalrous around ladies.

Texans generally have delighted in stepping into the boots the world holds ready for them. When all his life he has lived in routine anonymity among the home folks, the average Texan finds it pleasant to be welcomed as a minor celebrity by strangers abroad. Such a person plays the role expected of him most enthusiastically and often convincingly. There are, to be sure, other Texans who simply have been irked by the reputation and are as bored by the Typical Texan as many outsiders are. They are the individuals who resent profoundly the still current belief that Texas is wild and its people woolly. But most Texans are still enthusiastically "Texan" about everything.

The Typical Texan enjoys good health today in spite of the best efforts of the image-breakers who are determined to spread the news that "the West ain't wild any more" and that Texans are really just average Americans, no more bellicose than anybody else and no less ignorant of "what a good place really is" than the millions who have always chortled at "Tex's" state pride. True enough, he is not popular with all comers. Not even his most devoted admirers argue that he is, by nature, guaranteed to be easy to live with. Perhaps few really definite personalities are perpetually congenial company. But regardless of individual reactions to the Typical Texan, a great company of people throughout the English-speaking world have wondered where he came from—and what qualities he possesses that have made him live in the public mind. About this, actual Texans are perhaps more curious than anybody, as well they may be, since they know that the Typical Texan was not born of Texans.

In the early days of Texas settlement it was right poor form to inquire into anybody's background. Too many newcomers came to Texas because, though its weather was hot enough, Texas would prove less hot for them than the settled communities they had pulled out of. Where a man came from was his own business. And he could make that pretty plain by presenting the inquisitor with the business end of a gun.

Today, Texans are not so touchy. The past is forgotten except in the ways in which legend keeps it alive. Now perhaps we can raise *the* question without anybody's reaching toward the holster on his hip.

Where did this character come from, anyway?

CHAPTER ONE

Peddlers, Gallants, and Backwoodsmen

LONG before anybody ever heard of Texans, or even suspected that a "Typical Texan" might one day arise, Americans swore that each of their nation's three big sections, the East, the South, and what was then the West, had a special breed of people all its own. Special, that is, in the sense of looks, personality traits, and ways of behaving—or, as some said, misbehaving. It was irritating to a lot of Americans to have to admit kinship to their countrymen across the river, or beyond the mountains, who were unlike what they should be. The words "uncouth" and "peculiar" have always been useful in discussing one's neighbors; they were especially so in America before the Civil War, during the years when the Typical Texan was flexing his young muscles and winning his spurs.

When the British traveler, Harriet Martineau, sized up the people in Washington, she agreed that the Americans were indeed a mixture of types. Inclined to deafness, she kept her eyes open on her trip through America. "The Southerners," she wrote, "appear to the most advantage, and the New Englanders to the least." The ease and frank courtesy of the men from the South, though touched with some arrogance, contrasted favorably, she felt, with the cautious, somewhat gauche, and too deferential air of the New Englanders.[1] Miss Martineau could spot a Yankee anywhere by his uneasy gait, which seemed proof to her that he moved constantly under the shadow of his inability to protect himself. But "the odd mortals that wander in from the western border," she said, were not a class at all. No one of them was exactly like his brother; however, all of them were far different from men in the rest of the country.

These sectional characteristics had become by 1845 the basic source of a native American humor. Today that humor has lost punch, since local consciousness characterizes Americans far less now than it once did, and it is difficult to see why the ways of one's neighbors ever seemed so comic. But even if the humor of the 1840's is not uproarious to us, it does show very well what reputation the people of one section had among those of another. The pictures of the parties concerned were probably never too accurate, but they were at least founded on truth. "The scheming Yankee, the wild Kentuckian, the generous Virginian, the aristocratic Carolina planter" were the main types at which the public laughed,[2] though of course that public laughed first at everybody else and last at itself.

The inveterate voyager up and down the Ohio and Mississippi rivers, Timothy Flint, became very familiar with a broad cross-section of American types. A former New Englander himself, Flint was perhaps more pro-Yankee than some others who had spent longer years in the West, but his impression of Yankees was similar to the general western opinion of them. On one river trip from Pennsylvania to Louisiana, Flint had many companions whom he termed exact samples of the general character of New England immigrants. They were "poor, active, parsimonious, inquisitive," and fully convinced that no country could equal the one which they had left behind.[3]

Yankee migrants were common enough on the western travel routes, but the New Englanders whom westerners knew best were peddlers like "Solon Shingle," "Jonathan," "Sam Slick," and "Solomon Swap" whom the popular "Yankee" actors, Dan Marble and George Hill, portrayed on western stages. A jingle in Wilson Flagg's *The Tailor's Shop*, published in 1844, ran:

> A man of the olden time is Jonathan
> In thrift a Jew, in faith a Puritan ...
> The social pleasures Jonathan eschews;
> Six days devotes to Mammon, of the seven,
> And one to God, to insure his claims for Heaven.[4]

Before his cart hove in sight, people in the average western and southern communities knew with a sinking feeling that the rattling sound presaged the arrival of a Yankee peddler with his load of sundry notions. The westerner thought of Yankees in terms only of trickery, deceit, and fraud; hence his common name for them was "eel-skins." The western folk hero, Davy

Crockett, bitterly resented the peddler's ability to sell himself and his worthless goods to the local women. Of all the "cursed Adam varmints" in creation, the Yankee peddler was the one Crockett tried hardest to avoid. Peddlers swarmed the whole valley of the Mississippi with their pewter watches and horn gun flints, their peppermint drops and essences, and they always played possum in time of danger. But their ribbons and "dashy trash" enabled them to make love to the girls with every advantage over the natives.[5] It was a crime and a shame, grumbled Crockett.

One of the period's popular writers of western fiction, John Hovey Robinson, seconded Crockett's motion. The wily Yankee peddler was a Methodist at Wesleytown, talked of "sins of omission and commission," Christian perfections and "sanctification"—and promptly sold a good sister a tin teapot for fifty cents.[6] At Morry-place the same peddler was a Universalist who spoke eloquently of "infinite love," "final restoration," "the absurdities of the orthodox," and "the many unfortunates who had been driven to suicide through belief in endless misery." He then sold his customer a ladle which she did not want—for two shillings. At Calvin-lane, the peddler was a devout Calvinist who waxed ecstatic on the "election of grace." At "Tom-Painville" he was a flaming infidel, extolling the Age of Reason and mocking the Bible. To him religious toleration was not only democratic but downright good business.

The peddlers traveling in the West were usually young men eager to reap their profits while they could. Dead set on making a sale, they scorned every other consideration. Imprudence, cunning, dishonesty were simply techniques in their trade. Often a peddler's income, like the safety of his skin, depended on his ability to travel fast. Instead of saying "Well" when you asked him how he was, he would usually answer, "Moving, sir!" for if his health was good, he was sure to be on the move.[7]

T. C. Haliburton's "Sam Slick," the slickest of all Yankee peddlers, confessed to the profession's wily ways. In Maryland where a Yankee was on trial, Slick asked a bystander why.

"Stealin'," said he.

"A Yankee?" Slick asked himself. That seemed impossible, since he had never heard of a peddler's being stupid enough to get caught in a trick. Slick could only scratch his head and murmur, in his disbelief: "I don't believe he's a Yankee."[8]

People thus came to take astuteness as a trait native to most Yankees, but one "Jonas" credited his training at "Yarvard Uniwarsity." "I went there tew carry a load of pine wood," said Jonas, "and one of the tewters—as I believe they call 'em— cheated me out of tew sents, clean cash, when he give me the pay." From then on Jonas never forgot the lesson of his tutor, and got back his original pennies a thousand times. "This going to collidge," he said, "larns a feller tew trade awful sharp."[9]

If a certain Virginia innkeeper had never before personally experienced Yankee cunning, he probably felt like a veteran after his brush with a peddler who stopped overnight with him. Prejudiced against peddlers in general, the innkeeper at last agreed to give this one a room on condition that the Yankee play him a typically Yankee trick. The peddler jumped at the chance. Next morning, Jonathan slyly included the bed cover among some other articles he was pressing the landlady to buy. The low price of the cover attracted the woman, and she insisted that her husband should buy it because it would match hers exactly. Jonathan pocketed his money, and was almost out of sight down the road when the host called after him that he had forgotten to play the promised trick. Jonathan shouted back: "O, never mind, you'll find it out soon enough."[10]

Timothy Flint indicated more clearly than anyone else the position which the Yankee, as a character type, occupied among westerners before the Civil War. Along the Ohio River and the routes generally followed by travelers from New England, stories about Yankee tricks were rife. The materials of Yankee deception included wooden nutmegs, pit-coal indigo, and gin made by putting pine knots in whiskey. Wherever Flint and his family applied for a night's lodging, the innkeepers asked if they were Yankees. When Flint answered "Yes," he invariably saw a "lengthening of visage," but his assuring them that he was a missionary usually convinced them that he was a safe risk.

Everywhere Flint heard tales of Yankee impositions, petty tricks, small thefts, and departures without paying bills.

Through "Sam Slick," Haliburton pointed out in 1855 the basic differences between the typical New Englander and the typical southerner. The southerners, said Sam, as proud and as "sarcy" as the British, call "us Eastern folk Yankees, as a term of reproach, because having no slaves, we are obliged to be our own niggers, and do our own work." And as New Englanders are intelligent, enterprising, and skilful, and therefore too often creditors of the luxurious people of the South, the southerners do not like "us the better for that, and not being Puritans themselves, are apt to style us scornfully, those d——d Yankees."[11]

The eastern attitude toward southerners was less crystallized than the southern and western impression of Yankees. The West and South both contained a hodgepodge of character types, and most natives had seen Yankees in person. On the other hand, the East rarely laid eyes upon southerners and westerners. One "Kentuckian," David Crockett, received ovations and the keys of many cities when he made his famous tour through the North in 1834, because, among other reasons, he was one of the few men from his section easterners had ever seen. Travel had not yet become a general American pastime, and most people, unless migrating, stayed at home. Hence, southerners and westerners seldom went East. To them, the East offered little recompense for the effort and discomfort involved.

For this reason, southerners left relatively little permanent impression on the people of New England. However, the period's humorous writings, published and read most widely in the East, pictured two well-defined southern types. The first was representative of the "uncouth" class of small farmers inhabiting the hills and hollows of the rural South. This type was featured by such authors as A. B. Longstreet, J. T. Thompson, J. G. Baldwin, and G. W. Harris. The second, which appeared in romantic novels by the Virginians, George William Bagby and John Esten Cooke, represented the class which Charles Sealsfield spoke of as "the off-spring of chivalrous Virginia and the Carolinas."

To the eastern mind, the "chivalrous Virginian" was most nearly typical of southern character. The lives of the landed gentlemen and the great southern statesmen—Jefferson, Madison, Mason, and especially George Washington—corroborated the eastern notion that the southerner spent his time at ease on some genial plantation, surrounded by many slaves and unlimited acres. The southern gentry itself actively appreciated and eagerly played up to this romantic impression. Unlike the easterners and the aggressive pioneers of the new West, southerners shunned progress and change and hoped only for the survival of the courtly society which their colonial forebears had left them. In tastes and manners, the southerner was romantically inclined. Wealthy southerners still practiced the graces of England and revered the chivalric world of Scott's novels for its real or imagined resemblance to their own. Americans accepted the portrait of the southerner as aristocrat, and the southerner himself was sure it was a perfect likeness.

This charming picture would doubtless have endured if the Negro slave had been less conspicuous in the background. The death rattle of southern gentility began when Harriet Beecher Stowe and the Abolitionists saw to it that the eastern public recognized how necessary slave labor was to the gracious southern way of life. At the approach of the Civil War the southerner's picture began to appear less courtly, less genteel, as his slaves came into sharper focus. The southern gentleman's ready hospitality and his gallantry, his traditional interest in culture and feudal sports looked shoddy against a sea of black faces. But throughout most of the early decades of the nineteenth century, before the evils of slavery obscured the often admirable civilization that the slave system made possible, Americans outside the South took the southerner as he wanted to be taken— as a semiromantic character who charmed others almost as much as he charmed himself.

One of the clearest pictures of the southerner through the eyes of an outsider appeared in the *Western Monthly Review* as early as June, 1828. The anonymous author remarked that the southerner was as proud of his native section as the Yankee was

of New England. Because of his sunny climate the southerner
had a characteristically tanned complexion. His erect and lofty
bearing made it obvious that he had become accustomed to
commanding an inferior race of human beings, his slaves. His
disregard of expense, his ardent spirit, his preference for his
own country, and his reckless lack of concern for consequences
marked him a southerner.[12]

The westerner was the American character type most closely
related to the Typical Texan. His section then lay west of the
Appalachians, extended from Tennessee to the Great Lakes,
and covered the central Mississippi Valley. Whether or not his
home actually lay within the boundaries of Kentucky he was
generally called a "Kentuckian."

Since Kentucky had furnished great droves of emigrants to
the regions bordering her and those to the west, she was often
spoken of as the "mother of the western states."[13] Her ways
formed the pattern of thought and action which became fash-
ionable throughout the West. To her people, Kentucky was the
epitome of all that was desirable as a homeland. Flint compared
the typically proud Kentuckian to the British warriors marching
into battle with a song—not a prayer—on their lips praising
English roast beef. "The Kentuckian, when about to encounter
danger, rushes upon it crying, 'Hurra for Old Kentucky'."[14] If
possible, the Kentuckian was even more proud of his home locality than were southerners and Yankees.

Foreign travelers and visitors from other sections of the
United States often entered the West with apprehensions. Most
of them had heard stories about the popularity there of shooting, biting, knifing, and eye-gouging. These reports, coupled
with the proverbial reputation of frontier dwellers for "rugged-
ness," had established the Kentuckian throughout the English-
speaking world as a pretty tough customer. Daniel Boone's fame
was to a great extent responsible for this notion. At Ravenna, in
1821, the poet Byron was greatly impressed with the western
tales told by an American traveler named Coolidge. Coolidge's
stories about Daniel Boone, especially, excited Byron so deeply
that he wrote him into his *Don Juan*. Nor was Byron the only

observer who found Boone the possessor of special ways. Boone caught the fancy of the world. His reputation for independence was epitomized in his famous grievance: "I had not been two years at the licks [in Missouri] before a d——d Yankee came, and settled down *within an hundred miles of me!!*"[15]

Fisticuffs were the favorite outlet for the natural exuberance of the American backwoodsmen. Bred under circumstances demanding the most perfect physical development, the young native Kentuckians were in general the largest breed Timothy Flint had ever seen. Their great size came to be among their most famous characteristics. In 1844 Joe Cowell, the popular comedian, considered it unnecessary to describe a tall man who sat next to him in a theater box in any other terms than that he was a "Kentucky-looking man." The backwoodsmen's energy was equally great. A contemporary guidebook notes that the name of Kentuckian was constantly associated with the idea of fighting, drinking, and gouging.[16]

Western fighters often compared themselves to alligators, and Robert Montgomery Bird, the novelist, considered the comparison completely appropriate. Like the Kentuckian, wrote Bird, the alligator delights, when the warmth of spring has brought his fellows from their holes and placed them basking along the banks of a swampy lagoon, to dart into the center of the expanse and challenge the whole field to combat. He roars, he blows the water from his nostrils, he lashes it with his tail, he whirls around and around, churning the water into foam; until having worked himself into a proper fury, he darts back to shore again to seek an antagonist.[17]

A Kentuckian wrote home while on a visit to New York that most people of the Atlantic states actually knew less about westerners than they knew about the Chinese. Most of them imagined a western backwoodsman to be a "kind of humanized Ourang Outang, recently divested of a tail."[18] He reported that when they saw westerners in Congress, for example, who knew how to stand gracefully and make gestures and speak correct English, easterners were filled with amazement.

Mrs. Frances Trollope admitted that whatever their moral characteristics might be, the Kentuckians were a very noble-looking race of men, their average height considerably exceeding that of Europeans, and their countenances appearing extremely handsome.[19] A Kentuckian in J. S. Robb's *Streaks of Squatter Life* belonged to this breed. He boasted that he was one of the people and "none of your stuck-up imported chaps from the dandy states, but a real genuine westerner—in short, a hoss!"[20]

It was just such hosses as this who made Davy Crockett and his flatboat counterpart, Mike Fink, into their own folk heroes. In the opinion of most westerners, Crockett bore a happy resemblance to themselves: "A roarer from the Salt Licks, chock full of fun and fight, fisting and feeling, frolic and friendliness, all united in one man."[21] Crockett's fame, following close after that of the fabled Daniel Boone, spread throughout the nation because he was the image most easterners accepted as typical of Kentuckians.

Crockett's reputation furnishes the best description now available of the Kentuckian as a character type before 1860. A review of *Col. Crockett's Exploits and Adventures in Texas* (1836) summarized the significance of the Crockett legend. Whenever a new race of men spring into existence, the review claimed, they require a metaphorical person to mirror forth their peculiarities to the world—a nucleus around which the floating traits and individual anecdotes of the land may form. Such a man was David Crockett, hunter and congressman from Tennessee. The backwoodsmen took the man, put him on a pedestal, adorned him with the best of their own abilities, their own achievements, and their own dreams—and so Davy Crockett, the folk hero, was born. The gods and older folk heroes hardly performed more wonderful deeds than Davy. He could grease the lightning and ride it through a canebrake. He could breast the rushing current of the Mississippi while towing a dozen steamboats with his teeth; he could whip his weight in cougars, grin whole menageries into convulsions, and scream the thunder dumb.[22]

A speech Henry Clay delivered in support of the War of 1812 is proof that the fighting fame of the Kentuckians was nation-wide. Clay's words were boastful but sincere when he proclaimed in the Senate that "the militia of Kentucky are alone competent to place Montreal and Upper Canada at your feet."[23]

Easy as it was to find Kentuckians, southerners, and Yankees, there was before the Civil War no typical *American*. The heterogeneous commonwealth of the United States had failed to produce a common denominator of character. Crèvecoeur's question, "What then is the American, this new man?" came sooner than it could be answered. And anyhow, who was to answer it? In Crèvecoeur's time, the American was a southern planter, a small farmer, a shopkeeper, a manufacturer, a sailor, a schoolmaster, a peddler, a backwoods hunter, a flatboatman, a circuit preacher, a migrant traveling westward, and rather a good deal more if one but looked closely. No American could answer Crèvecoeur's question objectively.

Americans needed to look closely and to learn the truth about each other, to discover, as one easterner did, that westerners were "really more moral" than the people of many old communities,[24] and that easterners were, as Crockett reported, more peaceful and harmonious "than any people I ever was among."[25] Perhaps the people of any one of the sections would have done well to embody a little more of the traits of the other two. New England could have done with a bit more chivalry, the South could have stood some "push," and no doubt more than one Kentuckian admitted privately that he could use a Yankee trick or two.

Only foreigners thought of the American as a single type. In the 1860's a broadsheet appeared in London, entitled "Sam Slick, the Yankee Pedlar," in which Sam was a happy combination of Yankee, Kentucky, and southern characteristics. The broadsheet read:

It isn't every day that you see a genu-ine Yankee doodle, I calculate! Oh, no! Now look at me. I'm cast iron all over, and pieced with rock. One of my blows is either sudden death or long sickness. If I was to hit a fellow, it would knock him into mortal smash, and it 'ud take about eternity to pick up all the pieces. We Yankees are a tarnation cute race; we make a fortune with the right hand, and lose it with the left. I'm half fire, half love, and a touch of the thunderbolt!

Sam said he could ride on a flash of lightning and catch a thunderbolt in his fist. He had the prettiest sister and the best shooting rifle in all Virginia, and challenged anybody to match him, "the most glorious, original, and never-to-be-forgotten smash-biler-bustin', free and enlightened nigger-whipping Pedlar as ever was raised, and no soft-sawder. So, go ahead!"[26]

At home one Christopher Clodpole, Esquire, an American farmer, published in his *The Clodpole Papers* a self-description that perhaps heralded the new day of the American type. In Whitmanesque terms ("I am large, I contain multitudes"), the author confided that he had encompassed in himself the traits of many sections, and had come close to being *the American man*. It was easy to see that he was special. He was strongly tinctured with wooden nutmegs and Yankee ingenuity and, having lived many years in Maryland, had a mixture of southern chivalry to boot. In short, he had a strong touch of New England, something of the droll, half-horse, half-alligator of Davy Crockett, with a spice of Sam Slick and the snapping-turtle. "Take me out and out, ladies and gentlemen, the world must concede that I am a downright curious old fellow."[27]

"Curious" was certainly the word for him, Yankees, southerners, and backwoodsmen agreed. And with that they went their separate ways.

CHAPTER TWO

Men from God's Country

AMERICANS have long been sure that they live in the best land on earth, whether their part of it is the middle of the desert or Times Square. Never were they more certain of this than during the period when the mythical man from Texas rode out of the West.

When the Typical Texan arrived, conditions were right to receive him. With his intense pride in his own locality, he came on the scene in an era when American patriotism was split between two camps. Once the colonists got over their love for England and the "old countries," they quickly developed an abiding affection for the new land. Deep as it was, this loyalty was double-faceted. To some outsiders it seemed astonishingly incongruous in a single heart; but Americans understood it and well knew that both facets were essential to their love of country.

If Frederick Jackson Turner, the historian, had contrived to write the "natural history of the American spirit" which he felt must some day be done, a serious part of his story would surely have dealt with the divided loyalty which Americans bestowed upon their homeland in the first half of the nineteenth century. By the 1820's, when Texas colonization was in full swing, the United States was only at last beginning to live up to its name. America, as a political entity, had come a long way from her feeble status at the close of the Revolution as a loose confederation of sovereign colonies. As early as 1812, when she felt constrained to fight another war with England, America—complete with a twenty-year heritage—had already equipped herself with a set of symbols signifying her oneness and her individuality.[1]

Washington, for all his roots in the plantation South, was a hero of all the American people. The flag with its stars and stripes betokened the union of states sprung from the Old Thirteen, but as an emblem its over-all value was something more. Wherever it appeared, on staffs above government buildings, at the heads of parades, on Fourth of July bandstands, it stood for an emotional unity in American attitudes. The "nation," a very real concept, was thus expressed in symbolic forms which all its citizens could understand.

But during the years leading up to the civil conflict over the vitality of that concept, the American citizen recognized another, more instinctive, allegiance as well. This was his devotion to his immediate home locality. On the rare occasions when he came in contact with a traveler from abroad he was, fervently, the proud American, loyal to his nation and to the principles upon which it was based. But foreign visitors like Dickens, Mrs. Trollope, and Harriet Martineau, for all the noise their reports created, were few, and America's common man seldom met a foreigner. Most of his contacts were with fellow Americans, who took his allegiance to and enthusiasm for the nation as much for granted as he did theirs. Except on patriotic occasions when he listened again to the swelling cadences of the Declaration of Independence, sang "The Star Spangled Banner," and proudly contemplated the subject of the song unfurled above him, the average American seldom felt deeply stirred by such an abstraction as the American nation.

His feelings for his home community affected him differently. Rare though his encounters with foreigners were, the American, regardless of his address, at times met firsthand the people of other American sections. This was especially true in the areas through which most of the migrants passed on their way west. Consequently, people living along the main travel routes in the South and West—the rivers, the post roads, the rocky traces through the mountains—often rubbed elbows with travelers from New England and points between. The easterner who stayed at home had much less chance to meet residents of other localities, since the main direction of travel was westward.

When Americans did have the opportunity to witness people whose homes lay at any distance from their own, they peered

at them as novelties, if not freaks. Their observers assumed them
to be representative of the people they had left at home. What
they could not see, they guessed at. Often they assumed the
worst—like Sam Slick, who laughed at "everything that wa'nt
Yankee."

The typical Yankee expounded at length on the wonders of
New England. It had a cold climate and rocky terrain, but it
suited him well enough. No matter where you met him, you
would know him in five minutes as a Yankee, from the way he
talked about home. Timothy Flint believed that with the exception of the Scotch, Yankees had more local pride than any other
people; at all events they advertised it more.

But the Virginian's affection for his home matched anybody's.
J. G. Baldwin discovered that it made no difference where the
Virginian went, he carried Virginia with him—perhaps not the
whole of it, but always the little spot he came from. The Virginian might *breathe* in Alabama or some other such place, but
he continued to *live* in Virginia. If he looked at the Mississippi
Delta, it reminded him of the James River "low grounds." If he
saw the Texas prairies, he thought of the meadows of Shenandoah.[2] When people emigrated from the "Old Dominion," their
neighbors were puzzled. Where better was there to go?

Davy Crockett was certain the Kentuckian's love for Kentucky was in a class by itself. Speaking for himself and all his
neighbors, he said: "Thar's no human flesh in all creation that's
so partial to home and the family circle, square, kitchen, barn,
log-hut, pigpen or fireplace as a Kentuckian."[3] Another Kentuckian explained such enthusiasm: "There's no place on the
universal 'arth like Kaintuck; she beats all out West, for pretti-
ness; and you might bile down creation, and not get such another state out of it."[4]

Attempting to paint for his congregation a clear picture of
heaven, one western preacher described it as a "fair Kentucky
of a place."[5] At least one slave liked the state so well that he
stoutly maintained that in climate, soil, and in every other
quality, Kentucky had no equal in the Union. Only freedom, he
declared, could improve it.[6]

Such intense local feeling was among the first things which struck visitors from the Old World. It was among the most powerful drives of Americans everywhere.

The English Mrs. Trollope found in conversing with Americans between 1827 and 1830 that if she spoke of anything as "odd," they would assure her vigorously that the point in question was common only to one place, and not at all typical of the whole country.[7] To Mrs. Trollope, the United States was a continent of almost distinct nations, each one certain that it outshone its neighbors. She discovered that well into the nineteenth century, long after the colonies had become states, the old pre-Revolutionary provincial feeling between them, and between the localities within them, was still strong.

But localism and nationalism, for all their apparent contradiction, are not necessarily opposites. In the United States they have been like the double barrels of a shotgun. During the Typical Texan's natal period localism was more emotional than political and so was important mostly from a domestic standpoint. Geography encouraged it, but localism remained strong because of the conviction of a locality's people that its special interests and cultural values set them apart. The fact that they were seldom conscious of any emotional ties to outsiders was no indication that they were weak in national allegiance. That loyalty, in spite of sectional differences, was the greatest strength of the nation. The United States covered such a vast territory that only the voluntary devotion of its far-flung citizens could have unified them into a single political community.

This was the atmosphere of American home loyalties which Texas entered in 1845. The tradition that sprang up in the United States about Texans was natural enough in a nation conscious of local peculiarities. The feeling was so widespread that it led to the creation of special names for the men from various states. The term "Yankee" was rarely broken down more specifically, but "westerner" and "Kentuckian" frequently were. Though to green outsiders the people throughout the section were alike, residents of almost every western state came to be known to each other by special nicknames. For example, westerners rarely called the people of Tennessee "Tennesseeans"; more commonly they called them "Mudheads." Indiana "Hoosiers," Illinois "Suckers," Ohio "Buckeyes," Missouri "Pukes" or "Pikes," Michigan "Wolverines"—such names were long in vogue throughout the West, though to a Yankee they seemed irrelevant. The people were all Kentuckians to him.

But to a westerner the differences between one and another were sometimes immense. Davy Crockett was an authority on local western traits. In his opinion, the "Pukes" were "the most all sickenin' ugly critters" that the western land could breed and turn out. "Now I boast," Crockett said, "of being too ugly to get out of bed arter sunrise, myself, for fear I'd scare him back again, but then I an't sickly ugly; the Puke is so etarnally so, that his own shadow always keeps behind him, for fear that his all-spewy lookin' face would make it throw itself up." The Pukes, Crockett contended, "never look each other in the face but once a year, an' that's in the spring, when they want to vomit off their surplus bile."[8]

The Hoosiers, like the Pukes, were "a different class o' human natur altogether." Crockett described them as "half taller an' bristles, an' so all-sweaten fat and round, that when they go to bed they roll about like a cider barrel in a cellar." Therefore they were always obliged to keep a Negro on each side of them to hold them still. When they woke up, they had to fasten down their cheeks before they could open their eyes.[9]

The drinking talents of the Suckers became legendary. Suckers were the thirstiest people Crockett had ever seen. "Now I," he declared, "can swoller a Lake Superior o' lightnin' water, meanin' whiskey, in a superior fashion—but when I do, it lasts me till I git dry agin; but a Sucker never takes time to get dry, for he hangs to a bottle like a buzzard to a hoss bone, an' if he ever lets go, it's because his tarnal legs let go of his body."[10]

Crockett found the Michigan Wolverines by far the oddest bunch of all. The chaps from the Wolverine state were the "all-greediest, ugliest, and sourest characters" in Uncle Sam's whole territory. They were, by nature, like their wolfish namesakes, always so hungry that they bit at the air, and hung their under lips, as if they'd jump right into you, and, without salt, swallow you whole.[11]

To Crockett, no spot and no people could be described as merely different from all others; each was the "oddest," the "queerest," or the "all-fired beatin'est" on earth. He swore that the folks at New Orleans were the queerest mixture of "all creations' population that can be found in or about any part o' this here round-shouldered globe." They were about half Yankee, half "Monsieur," half Spanish, half Portuguese, half Indian, half "Nigger," with some shark and alligator thrown in.[12]

A century ago a state's name was often used as a nickname for its people. Aboard an American ship in the Caribbean, Lady Emmeline Wortley noticed this novel use of state names. Through her skylight, she constantly heard shouts like these:

"Indiana, come give us a song right away, and Alabama will join."

"No, it is Louisiana's turn."

"Where's Texas? Is he coming on deck?"

"Wall, I jist calc'late he ain't agoing to do nothing else; there he comes, too, with Michigan and Arkansas."[13]

Today, except in the case of the Texan, who is often called "Tex" or "Texas" away from home, such designations are rarely used, though the word "Okie" is not unknown. Recently, the juke boxes crooned a popular song about "Tex" and "Okie" and their buddy, "Arkie."

Whether you called the American "Hoosier," "Indiana," "Maine," or "Tex," he was, in his own opinion, among the chosen. In the community where he lived the people were superior in manners, and their land was so richly blessed with natural advantages that it made other places look sick. No wonder he called it God's country.

CHAPTER THREE

El Dorado—for Heroes or Rascals?

THE comedian, Peter Lind Hayes, has said that every Texan dreads to die because he will have to leave Texas to go to heaven. In the nineteenth century there was a saying that he was already in hell where he ought to be. Until long after Texas joined the Union, people in the United States often thought, or at least said, that Texas was another haven of iniquity which the Devil had specially reserved. One of them put it this way:

> When every other land rejects us,
> Here is a land which freely "takes us."[1]

Virginians once claimed that any man who disappeared from the Old Dominion had gone either to hell or to Kentucky; a later generation of Americans said, "Hell or Texas." Whatever it was, paradise or perdition, people flocked to Texas.

When the tide of Texas immigration rose high after 1821, it could be observed that all three of America's great sections were feeding the stream. From the first, the new arrivals poured in large numbers from New England, the Old South, and the Kentucky-Tennessee West, with the nearer southern areas predominating. Between 1825 and 1831 only one-eighth of the eight hundred-odd immigrants registered for settlement in Texas came from the Atlantic states.[2] But New England did furnish an important share; witness the *Cincinnati American,* which said in 1830 that thirty wagons had recently passed through the city bound for Texas.[3]

The great majority of migrants came from the regions closer to Texas. Awareness of this fact went far in fostering the public's conception of Texan character. For example, New Yorkers seeing daily newspaper references to Texas affairs were influenced in their impressions by reading that the West was a heavy contributor to settlement in the new territory. New York and the East, familiar with the Kentuckian as tall and rangy and full of fight, were sure that Texans were the same, when they learned that many of the new settlers were former Kentuckians. The *New York Star* noticed in 1835 that "a large force, much of which will be of the 'half-horse, half-alligator' race, will soon be collected in Texas. . . . The Texians are mostly muscular, powerful men, and great marksmen; and whether at a distance with the rifle, or in close combat, they will be terrible."

The East read, too, that many southerners were moving to Texas. Though the plantation class supplied only minor numbers in the immigrant stream, eastern readers assumed that the southerners who went to Texas were aristocratic and chivalrous. As they saw it, it was southern blood that gave the Texan his chivalry.

Actually, the southerners who went to Texas were for the most part common people, not aristocrats. The frontier was no place for a southern gentleman—or for a "gentle" man from anywhere. The raw frontier was not the healthiest place for the Sam Slick breed, either. On the other hand, the rough "Kentuckian" was made of the stuff that was sure to succeed in Texas. Moving there, he met no new obstacles. Kentucky and Tennessee had seen Indian disturbances within the memories of the men who left those states to settle beyond the Sabine. The Texas Revolution gave the Kentuckians a new enemy, the Mexicans, but this was no novel problem for them. The Kentuckians were "chock full" of fighting experience, and prowess learned along the Ohio and Cumberland thus gave the new Texan, or neo-Kentuckian, confidence along the San Jacinto and the Rio Grande. Stay-at-homes in the East realized all this; moreover, they took it seriously in devising a picture of the Typical Texan. Yankee characteristics, be it noted, were completely ignored.

In the 1840's two commentators on Texas affairs, A. B. Lawrence and F. B. Page, anticipated with pleasure the movement of emigrants from Europe and all sections of the United States to Texas where they would become friends, forgetting all their local feelings, "and making no other distinctions than grow out of character and talents."[4] They looked forward to the happy day when the "lordly Carolinian and chivalrous Georgian—and the independent Virginian, and the noble and free-hearted Kentuckian . . . and the hardy and enterprising New Englander, will here make common cause together—assemble on one common ground—rally round the standard of one common country, guided by one star to a common destiny, and a common glory."[5]

The people who settled Texas did indeed in time make "common cause together" and did forget all their former local feelings. But the being whom the public took as representative of the product of the southwestern melting pot was hardly the character Page and Lawrence had in mind. His Yankee blood seemed to have become so diluted that nobody could ever tell he had any. Except in the chivalrous ways he displayed around women, the same appeared to have happened to the heritage he had received from the South. The Typical Texan whom the public accepted looked, talked, frolicked, and fought like the men of "Old Kaintuck."

There were plenty of reasons, from the start, why non-Texans conceived of Texans in terms of the chesty backwoodsman. The fact that the earliest famous Texans—Jack Hays, Ben Milam, Ben McCulloch, Sam Houston, and David Crockett—all came to Texas from the Kentucky West supported the logic of the conception. It was unimportant that, actually, most Texans came originally from the South, not from the Kentucky West. The Kentucky personality was a "natural" for Texas.

As virgin country, quite apart from the character of the people who settled it, the American West has maintained a special significance. Its spirit has dominated the thinking of the New World. To men living east of the frontier[6] the West has beckoned as the promised land, a haven of hope that repeatedly called the adventurer. Whether it was the Mohawk and Shenandoah valleys of the colonial period, or the trans-Allegheny West of the early nineteenth century, or the great region comprising the Mississippi and the Rocky Mountains of a later date, the West has stirred the imagination throughout the nation's history. D. W. Brogan, from his vantage point in England, explains the feeling this way: "The American sees the sun move from the ocean inland; his evening view over the Atlantic is

gray and grim, while to the west the land is bright."[7] Archibald
MacLeish sees the West as always having offered promise:

> East were the
> Dead kings and the remembered sepulchres:
> West was the grass.[8]

Many Americans were captivated by exactly that, the new
world of grass and beckoning prairies, even if they disapproved
of the people who were settling there. They emphasized the
great potentialities which the land offered to men intelligent
enough and tenacious enough to develop it. Some viewed this
New West as the long-awaited "Passage to India." Others
thought of it as the future stronghold of a great American empire. Still others, less orderly in their thought, simply "cut stick
and lit out" for gold—or wanted to. Whatever he thought specifically about it, the average American maintained a freedom of
spirit unhampered by the shortcomings of life in the settled
areas, because he knew there was a West to go to. Even if he
never contemplated a migration westward himself, the American in the East enjoyed, consciously or otherwise, the feeling
that there was still room for his nation to expand. The conviction that vast opportunities abounded in the West was a prime
factor in America's essential optimism during the eighteenth
and nineteenth centuries.

In addition to the West's romantic appeal as a region, the
western American person often seemed engaging and stimulat-
ing. Like Byron, Thomas Carlyle delighted in tales of men in
the American wilderness. When in 1847 Theodore Parker, the
Boston divine, visited Carlyle at his home, the Englishman
pumped him for stories of the West. To oblige, Parker drew a
rough sketch of Jim Bowie, the Texan martyred at the Alamo.
Carlyle listened in an "ecstacy of delighted wonder; rubbed his
hands in a sort of savage glee," betraying in his whole countenance the intense interest he took in Parker's stories.[9]

The men who went west were interesting adventurers. Their
contemporaries sometimes praised their bravery; at other times
they called them foolish wanderers or worse. In the settled
United States, the homebodies questioned the sense of leaving

behind a life of law and order. "Solid" citizens often wondered whether ambition or simple expedience was the reason for the trek west. Often the man with the itchiest foot was a known absconder. The pious and the law-abiding maintained that the real heroes stayed at home on the job and faced up to the problems of decent living. In their opinion the West was for ne'er-do-wells who had buckled under the strain of Godly living and respectability. Let them go west and good riddance.

An equal number of people felt quite the opposite. They looked toward the sundown and dreamed. Excitement was in the air. The Westward Movement was one of history's great adventures, and they knew it. If they could not join up, the faithful individuals remaining in the cities and on the farms of their fathers shared in spirit all the perils and infinite challenges of the great migration.

As a part of the West, Texas enkindled two schools of stridently voiced opinion. Her settlers provided matter for constant debate. There were people who liked the hardy clan. In 1848 *Holden's Dollar Magazine* asserted that "next to the French Revolution, there is no subject so replete with romantic interest as Texan adventures."[10] Ten years later, a traveler insisted that Texas offered splendid material for the wildest yarns. The *New York Mirror* in 1836 considered Texas an "Eldorado of modern hopes" where the skies set the only limits. But others, like Horace Greeley, who represented the grievances of the anti-annexationists, sneered that Texas was a "den of thieves," sworn to perpetuate domestic slavery. Greeley claimed that the men of influence and office in Texas were the rejected criminals of better lands. Texas, in his estimation, was the "rendezvous of rascals for all the continent," red with the blood of violence and reeking with dissoluteness.[11]

Edward Everett Hale, at least as fearful of a spreading Texas influence in the United States as Horace Greeley, came up with one possible solution to the problem when he seriously urged New Englanders, en masse, to settle in Texas. A call to arms, the title of his pamphlet proclaimed the urgency of the situation: *How to Conquer Texas Before Texas Conquers Us.*[12]

In a later work, Hale demonstrated the ubiquity of the famous reference to Texas in the abbreviation, "G. T. T." More than a generation ago, Hale wrote in 1877, one of the commonest jokes said that when a debtor or any ne'er-do-well had to leave home, he chalked upon his door the letters G.T.T. These letters were not mysterious. They were everywhere understood to mean, "Gone to Texas."[13]

Popular imagination had it that the folks who went to Texas were all people with a "past." The facts were often far different, but the opponents of the mass migration held to their belief that the settlers were outlaws and "degenerates." Actually, most of the early settlers were decent enough men seeking homes for their families. Stephen F. Austin, the number one Texas colonizer, insisted that immigrants present written evidence of unblemished character.[14] But the fiction, more colorful than the fact, quickly spread that above all else Texas was, in J. O. Pattie's phrase, an "Elysium of rogues."[15] Many stock slurs of the day contained references to the character of the would-be Texas settler. For example, a wellerism in the *Spirit of the Times* for June 29, 1839, expressed one prevalent attitude toward the motives behind much movement to Texas: " 'Ven are you going to Texas?' as the boy said to the man vot wanted to get trusted." There was also the story of the distressed newcomer to Texas who asked a lawyer for advice. The lawyer replied: "My friend, this is very serious business. My counsel is that you leave this place before sundown."

"Leave!" said the newcomer. "Where'll I go? Ain't I in Texas now?"[16]

Alexander Sweet told of a conversation around a campfire, in which various men were telling why they came to Texas—one because he had killed a man, another because he had forged some checks. A former preacher, now a gambler, said nothing. The others begged him to tell why he came.

"I don't care to say anything about it. Besides, it was only a trifle. None of you would believe me, anyhow."

"Out with it, man, did you shoot somebody?" asked one of the group.

"No, gentlemen, I did not. But since you want to know so bad, I'll tell you. I left Kentucky because I did not build a church."

This was an unexpected answer. They insisted on hearing the rest.

"Well, gentlemen, you see a Methodist congregation raised $3,000 and turned it over to me to build a church—and I didn't build the church. That's all."[17]

Slurs like this were felt keenly in certain quarters. A reviewer of Mrs. Mary Austin Holley's *Texas* welcomed her refutal of the common attitude, which was, in his opinion, "an exaggeration, if not gratuitous slander."[18]

But the ugly name was the one that stuck. Whether or not Austin was right in declaring that the disparagement of Texas character originated with those banished from Texas as "unfit," the "renegades and ruffians" reputation gained an early and lasting currency in the United States. If Texas was not really a great "valley of rascals," as a Whig campaign broadside said it was in 1844, the notion was an extremely hard one to kill. In 1853 the folk historian, J. G. Baldwin, observed that citizens of any older country are prone to rate the people of newly settled areas as trifling inferiors. Commiseration on the part of the old-sters for the shortcomings of their upstart neighbors out west was a very natural sentiment: "It is flattering to pride, and it tickles the vanity of senility." Eastern deprecation of the man-ners of the West and Texas was evidence of the easterner's be-lief that his own nobly formed society had arrived at respectable maturity. Obviously any society which differed from his own must be less worthy. Assuming that civilization in a new country like Texas could exist only at a rudimentary level, the East opined that people willing to migrate there must be barbarians satisfied with anarchy. Baldwin labeled the criticism as just an-other variety of the old game of passing the buck. In America "the Bostonian looks down upon the Virginian—the Virginian on the Tennesseeian—the Tennesseeian on the Alabamian—the Alabamian on the Mississippian—the Mississippian on the Louis-ianian—the Louisianian on the Texian—the Texian on New Mexico, and we suppose, New Mexico on Pandemonium."[19]

The objections to Texas annexation were principally based on the fact that Texas would become a slave state. But the shady reputation of her people was a sizable stone in the wall raised between them and American citizenship. In his diary entry for August 20, 1845, Philip Hone, one of New York's Four Hundred, deplored the imminence of annexation. He was profoundly alarmed because the men composing the Texas legislature which had agreed to the American annexation terms were of dubious political principles, loose character, and "desperate fortunes."[20] Hone had been disturbed as much the year before by the Americans favoring annexation. He had attended an anti-annexation meeting in New York and had been appalled when it was broken up by a gang of "prize-fighters and pardoned felons" who hissed, groaned, and shouted, "Hurrah for Texas!"[21]

A vast group in America joined Greeley and Hone in disparaging the principles, as well as the character, of the Texans. Many who otherwise might have admired the Texans' tenacity in fighting the Mexicans scoffed at the idea that Texas' grievances against Mexico were sound. The *Western Monthly Magazine* for April, 1836, approved the Texan demands for better political and religious opportunities, but ridiculed those Americans who were daily going to Texas, as one patriot put it, "to fight for my rights."[22] The championing of "patriotic principles" was wholly beside the point. Men went to Texas fully aware of the instability of the Mexican government and of the complete absence of faith or principle shown by those who were to be their rulers.[23] To some, the Texas Revolt was nothing but an organized run for plunder. William Ellery Channing, in a letter to Henry Clay in 1837, said he was convinced of it; the zeal for freedom which had stirred and armed so many Americans to fight for Texas "turns out to be a passion for unrighteous spoil."[24]

Newspapers throughout the East furthered the impression that future Texans would be the spawn of outcasts. During the Texas Revolution, the years 1844 and 1845, and the Mexican War period, papers of all the major eastern cities were packed with references to Texas. In the years immediately before and after annexation, newspapers seldom missed mentioning something about Texas, either its peculiar populace, its annexation, its fisticuffs with mother Mexico, or its own domestic rifts.

Since Texas affairs were so closely related to American politics, the newspapers naturally evinced an editorial interest in Texan character. The Manhattan papers—the *Sun,* which James Gordon Bennett accused in 1836 of jeering Texas and bravoing Mexico, the *Morning Express,* and the *Dispatch*—were all violently anti-Texas in policy. The *Dispatch* carried articles decrying the "utterly appalling" number of homicides, murders, and assassinations in Texas. The *Morning Express* became extremely critical of Texan character during the anti-Polk campaign which it supported in 1844. The *Spirit of the Times,* always partial to western character, denounced in 1838 the eagerness of "our brethren of the type at the North" to misrepresent the Texans as "wicked and desperate."

But the most virulent journalistic attack ever waged on the Texans appeared in Greeley's paper, the *Clay Tribune:* "Any great extension of our territory," Greeley wrote, "would probably ruin us; but were it otherwise, what kind of an addition will Texas be?" What motive would decent Americans have for wedding themselves to a populace whose "law is might, whose liberty licentiousness, whose religion not at all?"[25]

Actually, Greeley was stretching a point when he scoffed that there was no law in Texas, as "Three Legged Willie" Williamson could have proved. Appointed by Sam Houston as district judge for the Upper Brazos, Williamson let the community know how things were going to be, after some of the citizens had informed him that they wanted none of Houston's courts there. At his table, Williamson placed a rifle at one elbow and a pistol at the other and declared: "Hear ye, hear ye, court for third district is either now in session or by God somebody's going to get killed."[26]

Despite all outcries, sympathy for the Texans and admiration for their deeds increased vigorously during the green years of the Texan Tradition. Observers of the Texas-Mexico conflicts, whether they were for or against annexation, often broadcast their belief that the Texas revolt from Mexico was in miniature a restatement of their own hallowed break with tyrannical England. The historian H. S. Foote reported in 1841 that the "Philo-Texan spirit" was more predominant in the South and West than elsewhere, but that even in the land of the Pilgrims many enlightened friends of "Moral and Intellectual Advancement" felt bound to patronize the efforts of those who, like themselves, desired enthusiastically that the triumphs of science and virtue be carried forward into "the dark abodes of Barbarism and vice."[27] In 1836 the *New York Herald,* hailing the Texan victories in the Revolution, printed a poem which voiced a popular attitude:

> Men of Texas! from the North—
> Children of your fatherland—
> We would fling our numbers forth
> Thus to hail your gallant band.[28]

The motives of a Captain John Sowers Brooks for going to Texas from Virginia to fight in the Revolution were typical. Speaking of that war as similar to the glorious struggle of "Seventy-six," Brooks believed that many youths of his country had inherited enough of the spirit of their forefathers to induce them to procure, as he had done, a musket and a hundred rounds of ball cartridge, and join "the holy crusade against priestly tyranny and military despotism."[29]

Presenting a gift to a Kentucky volunteer about to leave for Texas, Miss Martha V. Shain of Louisville said, "Accept sir, a brace of pistols to be used in defence of Texian liberty. . . . I place them in your hands, feeling assured that you will . . . maintain the reputation of our country."[30]

Just as the famous "Twin Sisters" cannons, two iron six-pounders, had been given to the Texas army by sympathizers in Cincinnati, the San Jacinto battle flag was the gift of the ladies of Newport, Kentucky. Its motto read: "Liberty or Death." When the news of the San Jacinto victory reached Cincinnati on May 17, 1836, a theater audience received it with three rounds of applause. The orchestra struck up "Hail Columbia," and the crowd renewed its cheers. James Gordon Bennett was sure, so intense was the rejoicing in New York, that more guns were fired in celebrating Houston's victory than in the battle itself.[31] He predicted for Sam Houston a place in immortality beside Washington as an American hero.

And so the argument went on: on the one hand, the Texans were a paltry lot sure to bring shame and corruption into the American family circle; on the other hand, they were a "young hero people, . . . coming out of the forests, walking in light, and clothed in strength, and advancing in manliness up to our altars."[32] But as for the Typical Texan himself, he grew up oblivious to the argument. Half wild, half worthy, he worried not at all about his good name.

TEXAN MOUNTED MILITIA

Illustrated London News (1842)

"The Texans are a young and gallant people . . . enterprising,
ambitious, and bold."

CROCKETT AT THE ALAMO

Crockett's Almanac
(New York, 1848)

"When my amminition war gone, I give 'em the breech of my muskitt."

DEATH OF CROCKETT

Crockett's Almanac
(New York, 1848)

". . . the crittur would as soon have faced a hundred live mammoths as to have faced Crockett at any time."

CHAPTER FOUR

The Big Three

THE TEXANS were indeed a tough lot; but a good deal of the argument about their true nature was only secondhand steam from the newspapers. Americans, by and large, supported the newspaper opinion closest in line with their politics and allowed themselves to guess at the rest. Few outsiders ever saw Texans in the flesh, because Texans seldom left home; they knew a good place when they found it, they said. Only a small minority of the curious ever went to the trouble of sizing up Texans on their home grounds.

In 1845 Francis Copcutt asserted that while by that time everyone had a definite idea about Texan character, few if any people in America knew anything accurate about it. Copcutt wrote an article for the *Knickerbocker* which he hoped would set people straight. He chose as his subject a single Texan, Mirabeau B. Lamar, in order to answer once and for all the question, "What are the Texians?" Some years earlier a New York paper had said that Lamar was the only man in Texas who possessed a character "unstained by villainy of some sort or other."[1] Copcutt disagreed, and he told his readers why. He knew the Texans from firsthand experience, and he contended that Lamar's physical bravery and moral fortitude were to a great extent typical of them all. Like most Texans, Lamar was blessed with an "indomitable dare-devil courage, and that ready ability to do, on the spur of the moment, when the danger becomes more imminent" what others would have had to ponder long about.[2]

The general public lacked opportunity to examine individual Texans as closely as Copcutt did. When noted Texans came east, few people got close enough to them to learn much about them. The only impression the man in the crowd gained was a visual one. To him the Texan was a big fellow, bluff and hearty. The

35

bearing of such famous figures in Texas history as David Crockett and Sam Houston encouraged belief in the East that all Texans were rawboned specimens of muscular manhood.

From the time of Crockett's first appearance in 1827 as a Tennessee congressman scores of newspapers, finding him colorful copy, had spread his fame in stories. These went to extremes, and were either highly exaggerated or subdued, depending on the editor's attitudes toward Crockett and Jacksonian Democracy. Crockett's own pen, with much help from collaborators, furthered his national reputation with his first three autobiographical books,[3] *Sketches and Eccentricities of Col. David Crockett* (1833), *Narrative of the Life of David Crockett* (1834), and *A Tour to the North and Down East* (1835). Widely popular, they ranked a little behind the "Crockett" almanacs in spreading his fame. These three books appeared before Crockett linked his name with Texas. Wherever seen, he created a stir—if not a sensation. As the "Coonskin Congressman" he was unique. His ability to talk in picturesque phrases assured him an audience wherever he went, and his talk was often repeated because of its "pithy center."[4] In Congress the "Kentuckian" attracted attention at once, in spite of the fact that he usually wore an ordinary black suit instead of a hunter's buckskins. It was simply that his demeanor was compelling. He breathed the spirit of the great outdoors. Physically, Crockett looked like a westerner, and needed no special trappings to prove his title. Because no one like him had ever appeared in office, he aroused curiosity even in people who normally took no interest in politicians.

At a Washington performance of Paulding's play, *The Lion of the West,* in 1833, Crockett attended as guest of the management and occupied a special box. While James H. Hackett, who played "Nimrod Wildfire," and Crockett bowed to each other, the theater rang with cheers. In bowing to Hackett, Crockett acknowledged Hackett's position as the most popular interpreter of Kentucky character on the stage.[5] In returning the courtesy, Hackett paid tribute to Crockett's national reputation as the typical westerner. Such fanfare won him renown and was good for the theater's box office. It is small wonder that at this same time Crockett was planning a similar visit to a Philadelphia theater as the manager's guest, "due honors to be tendered, and all bills to be paid."[6] Later in the year when he was an invited guest of the National Theater in Boston, Crockett was reported to have looked, in his black suit, more like a clergyman than a fighter. Yet he excited in the audience an interest which could not have been greater unless they had foreseen that within two years this hero would "lie a stark and bloody corpse . . . surrounded by a holocaust of alien foes in the memorable Alamo."[7]

Crockett's fame and popularity throughout the East would have influenced the Texan Tradition even if he had never joined the Alamo's defenders. After Daniel Boone, Crockett was America's liveliest idea of western character. Aware that a large proportion of Texans had migrated from Crockett's West, easterners naturally imagined the Texan in terms of Crockett's legendary character and appearance. When Crockett joined the exodus to Texas in 1835, he tied forever the bonds that would link his name with the Typical Texan. Crockett symbolized not only the mood of his world, but many of its activities. The most famous American ever to migrate to Texas, he went there for a very common, a very widely understood reason. He had been thwarted in one of the great aims of his life, re-election to Congress. Like the vast group of "G. T. T." migrants, Crockett saddled kit and caboodle and rode off to Texas to start over. Though the actual David died too soon for the Texas chapter in his life to be a long one, the legendary Davy entered one of his greatest and most colorful periods when he climbed the west bank of Red River.

Crockett took along to Texas not only his disappointment, his fighting tools, and his resentment of Mexicans, but also the whole force of the Crockett reputation which thus became the bottom stone in the Texan Tradition. If there was ever any doubt that the Texans were from the same mold as Kentuckians, Crockett's death as a Texan in the Alamo removed for all time that final reservation. He there became identified fully with the Texans who died with him. Thereafter, the publications and the stories that spread his fame frequently treated Crockett as a Texan. Indeed, in this literature he became the prototype for all the heroes of that area and time. The fact is that the typical man of the Lone Star came only slowly to exhibit traits even slightly different from the pattern which the Crockett of folklore set for him.

The man best known in the United States for diligent sponsoring of Texan settlement was Stephen F. Austin, "the father of Texas." Considering first his efforts to make Texas a peaceful colony of Mexico, and later his determined leadership in freeing her, Austin deserves the title. But Austin was not endowed with a personality calculated to excite many people's imaginations. In almost all respects, he was everything admirable that a sober founding father should be. He possessed only one major negative quality, but it was a fatal one. In his personal makeup he was, compared to the frontier flamboyance that surrounded him, dull. Hence, his people never made him their hero. On the other hand, Crockett was, through the tradition enlivening his name and through his dramatic and heroic death at the Alamo, the complete summation of frontier qualities that formed the Texans' ideal. If Austin was the father of Texas, David Crockett was the father of the Typical Texan.

However later Texans like Sam Houston and Big-Foot Wallace may have impressed observers in the older states, their kinship in personality to the fabled Crockett was the quality which best established their juncture with the Texan Tradition. Sam Houston, like Crockett, had gained fame or notoriety in America long before he left for Texas. His mysterious divorce, his resigning the Tennessee governorship, and his connections with Andrew Jackson had combined to make his name well known. Even before he joined actively in the Texan Revolt, Houston's prophecy of 1834, made during a drinking bout with Edwin Booth, had been widely quoted: "Yes, yes! I am made to revel yet in the halls of the Montezumas."[8]

Unlike Crockett, Houston fell short as a teller of tall tales. His effect on easterners was a visual one. As early as 1818, when he was twenty-five, Houston had already become aware of his commanding figure and powerful personality. When Noah Ludlow, then director of the Nashville Dramatic Club, cast him as a drunken porter, Houston bellowed: "What? low comedy? Sam Houston in low comedy. Great God! . . . Surely you're not serious? . . . By the Eternal, sir, the people will hiss me." Catching his breath, Houston roared, "Look here, Ludlow, if the people hiss me tonight, I'll shoot you tomorrow."[9] Wherever Houston went in the East, he exhibited his command of histrionics. In 1830 Washington beheld him dressed "in the costume of the wigwam." For every occasion he had a new blanket, and the metal ornaments on his buckskin coat tinkled as he walked.[10]

Physically, he far outshone Crockett. His friend, Andrew Jackson, admiring the figure Houston cut in leather breeches and a Mexican blanket, expressed it memorably. He thanked God that there was one man, at least, "whom the Almighty had had the making of, and not the tailor."[11] Houston stood well over six feet in his stocking feet. About 1836 the *New Orleans Bee* praised Houston's "manly and noble countenance rarely surpassed among men." When Houston visited the fashion centers, Newport and Saratoga, both cities beheld him in "full sartorial glory."[12] When Houston was enthusiastically received at the New York City Hall in December, 1846, the *Morning Express* reported: "As General Houston was a good deal the tallest man in the crowd, as well as the most distinguished, he was particularly 'the observed of all observers'." Standing in the center of the room, he greeted the public with a long cloak, lined with scarlet velvet, hanging from his shoulders.

When Houston joined the Senate, he continued to sport his singular wardrobe. His dress was always peculiar, though consistently becoming to him. Its notable features were a military cap and a short cloak of blue broadcloth lined in blood red. People occasionally saw him in Washington wearing a "vast and picturesque sombrero and a Mexican blanket."[13]

From his appearance the East would certainly have deduced that Houston was no retiring sort. If he failed to brag in Homeric language of his own abilities as had Crockett before him, few of his observers doubted the scope of those capacities. At his New York reception the *Sun* noted the bravery, independence, talent, and democracy stamped on his face. The most famous Texan to appear in the East since the annexation, Houston fitted perfectly the conception easterners had begun to form of Texans; and his presence served to chisel that image even more boldly.

As the hero of San Jacinto, Houston received enthusiastic support in many American newspapers from the earliest news of his victory over Santa Anna. America's enthusiasm for him matched that of a Texan who in 1837 toasted: "Sam Houston: the man who is contented to be called Sam, and who has proved a Sam-son to the enemies of Texas."[14] The *New York Herald,* with its editor's usual fervor, proclaimed that *"as sure as the sun is in Heaven, Samuel Houston will be the President of the United States. . . .* A man greater than Greece or Rome ever produced—equal to Washington."[15] The *Boston Times* praised Houston's notable feat of capturing Santa Anna up a tree. "Even the great Crockett could hardly have done better." Santa Anna's tribute to Houston at San Jacinto was widely quoted: "You have conquered the Napoleon of the South—he who could do that *is born to no common destiny."*[16]

In the Senate, where his vigorous oratory became famous, Houston spoke like the Typical Texan. In 1850 he defended the Texas Rangers' widely censured behavior at the Battle of Monterrey. Denouncing Zachary Taylor's criticism of the Rangers, Houston thundered: "Why, sir, two hundred and fifty rangers, if he had called them into service, would have repulsed any attempt that might have been made to cross the Rio Grande. . . . Five hundred Texian Rangers would have been more than enough to accomplish the object."[17]

Obviously, Houston's personal influence in furthering the Texan Tradition was great. Nothing about him was ordinary— his build, his dress, his bearing, his speech. After the Revolution, when he enjoyed his greatest fame in the United States, he was the cynosure of all eyes wherever he went, both through the force of his personality and because of his touted achievements

as the leader of the Texans against Mexico. In the Senate he set
a precedent in manner that has endured to the present in the
forceful figure of Tom Connally. Houston's great size, his aggressiveness, and his indomitable personality formed his chief public appeal. The fact that he was a known hero to the Texans
themselves helped greatly to establish him in the East as typical
of Texans in general.

Though in many respects Houston's actual importance in
Texas history is no greater than Austin's, big Sam always over-
shadowed Austin in Texas because he was endowed with the
kind of personality Texans valued most. In 1836, Austin received only 587 presidential votes compared to Houston's 5,119.
The capital city of Texas was named for Austin, it is said, so that
his name would not be forgotten completely.[18] Houston, however, has remained alive as a hero to the majority of Texans,
and to the rest of the country he comes close to typifying them
all.

Soon after the Mexican War the third member of the Big
Three in the legend's formation visited the East. William A. A.
"Big-Foot" Wallace had come to Texas from Virginia in 1837.
He was among the earliest Texans to discover, when he went
eastward, that a tradition was developing about men of his
adopted region. Like most Texans who came after him, Wallace
made no attempt to discredit the legend. Rather, where it suited
him, he delighted in playing the proffered role. And Wallace
was an early enough visitor in the East to be among the original
influences on the area's conception of Texans. He was one of the
first Texas Rangers to appear in person outside of the Southwest. Both his looks and his talk struck the people who met him,
whether American or foreign. While a prisoner of the Mexicans,
Wallace, whose six feet two inches towered over his captors,
had needed a new pair of shoes. He wore size twelve. None of
the shops in Mexico City could supply shoes of such dimensions,
so he was forced to buy leather and have a pair made. From
then on the Mexicans, amazed at the size of his feet compared
to their own, called him "Big-Foot."[19]

On his way east Wallace attended Dan Rice's circus in Cin-

cinnati. When the ringmaster offered ten dollars to anyone who
could ride his horse, Wallace, not willing "to see the horse come
off winner," stepped into the circle, told the ringmaster that he
could ride it, and sprang into the saddle. In a moment the fellow discovered, from the way he maneuvered, that Wallace was
going to "stick" him; so he made some excuse to take hold of the
bridle, and said to him in a low voice, "Where are you from?"

"From Texas," said Wallace.

"The d——l," said the ringmaster, "I'll give you twenty dollars
if you will let the horse throw you."[20]

In Virginia, Wallace's friends and relatives received him
heartily. But though they were anxious to make his time among
them pleasant, Wallace could tell from the start that they considered him a kind of "half-civilized savage that never could be
entirely tamed."[21] A few weeks after his arrival he attended a
ball given in his honor. The crowd was eager to see the "Wild
Texan," as they called him. Wallace soon caught on to the fact
that he was a curiosity, especially with the young ladies, who
plied him with questions about Mexico, Texas, Indians, and the
prairies. At first he answered all their questions truthfully; but
when he found that they doubted his facts, he "branched out,
and gave them some 'whoppers,' which they swallowed without
'gagging'." In answer to one young woman who asked him how
many horses he had ever seen in one drove, Wallace told her
thirty or forty thousand.

"Oh! now! Mr. Wallace," she said, "don't try to make game
of me in that way. Forty thousand horses in one drove! Well, I
declare you are a second 'Munchausen'."

"Well, then," said Wallace, "maybe you won't believe me
when I tell you there is a sort of spider in Texas as big as a peck
measure, the bite of which can only be cured by music."

"Oh, yes," she answered, "I believe that's all so, for I have
read about them in a book."[22] What book, she failed to say.

Among other whoppers he told the company, Wallace described the "Santa Fe," whose bite was worse than the tarantula's, for "the best brass band in the country couldn't cure [its]
sting." The monster had a hundred legs, with a sting in each one

of them, and fangs as big as a rattlesnake's. If you were stung
with its legs alone, you might possibly live an hour. If with all
its stings, perhaps fifteen or twenty minutes. But when it stung
and bit you at the same time, you first turned blue, then yellow,
and then a "beautiful bottle green." Then your hair all fell out
and your fingernails dropped off and you were "dead as a door-
nail in five minutes, in spite of all the doctors in America."[23]

"Oh, my! Mr. Wallace," said a woman, "how have you managed to live so long in that horrible country?"

"Why, you see," said Wallace, "with my tarantula boots made
of alligator-skin, and my centipede hunting-shirt made of tanned
rattlesnakes' hides, I have escaped pretty well; but these don't
protect you against the stinging scorpions, 'cow-killers,' and
scaly-backed chinches, that crawl about at night when you are
asleep! The only way to keep them at a distance is to chaw tobacco and drink whisky, and that is the reason the Temperance
Society never flourished much in Texas."

"Oh!" said the woman, "what a horrible country that must be,
where the people have to be stung to death, or 'chaw' tobacco
and drink whisky! I don't know which is the worst."

"Well," Wallace replied, "the people out there don't seem to
mind it much; they get used to it after a while; in fact, they
seem rather to like it, for they chaw tobacco and drink whisky
even in winter-time, when the 'cow-killers' and stinging-lizards
are all frozen up."[24]

A girl asked him if women were in much demand in Texas.

"I should think they were," he said. "The day the first young
woman came into our settlement there were fourteen Spanish
horses badly foundered on sedge-grass, by the young men who
flocked in to see her, from forty miles around." The next morning, Wallace reported, "she had seventeen offers of marriage
before breakfast." The Texas belle had a little trouble making
up her mind about which man to accept, but before she could
announce her decision one of them caught her up behind him
on his horse, rode off full speed in search of a priest, and forced
him to marry them on the spot. This seemed a good solution to
Wallace, because the girl was saved all further trouble on the

subject and she and her husband had lived happily ever since on one of the finest cattle ranches in the County of Karnes.[25]

Asked about mirages, Wallace was confused for a moment. Never having heard the word and completely ignorant of what the woman meant, Wallace told her he had seen at least a thousand of them. She was surprised to hear they were so common.

"Oh, yes," Wallace answered, "the last one I saw was just back of Santa Fe, and it stampeded when we got in about a quarter of a mile of it; and such a dust as was kicked up you never saw, for there hadn't been a drop of rain there in six months."

"Well, I declare," said a Miss Matilda. "I always heard that the mirage would disappear as you approached it, but never heard of one kicking up a dust before."

"No," said Wallace, "they don't in other countries, where the ground is kept wet by constant rain; but in Texas, you see, it is different."[26]

Big-Foot Wallace never sounded more like Davy Crockett than he did when he told how happy he was to leave Virginia for home. He said he never got to rights again till he returned to Texas and got into an Indian "scrimmage," and scalped one or two of them with "Old Butch." That night for the first time his appetite came back, and he ate six pounds of buffalo hump, a side of ribs, and a roasted marrow-gut, and ever since, Wallace said happily, "I have been 'as well as could be expected'."[27]

The first three famous Texans, Crockett, Houston, and Big-Foot Wallace, were three men of a kind. In physique, they were big; in language, they were bigger, and in all their ways, they were colorful. Of pride in Texas they had plenty. They were all top-notch men in battle—Houston as a commander, Crockett and Wallace as fighters to do the dirty work. No one man has come closer to being the individual embodiment of the Typical Texan than these three. Of the trio, Big-Foot Wallace's name looms largest, for he could talk taller any day than Sam Houston, and when he joined the Texas Rangers and began using their Colt revolver he learned a better way to fight than Davy Crockett's.

Six-Gun Men

As a group, the Texas Rangers became as famous as the Big Three, the most celebrated Texans in America. Certain of their leaders—Jack Hays, Dan Drake Henrie, and Samuel Walker—were touted as champions on their western home ground and as celebrities when they visited the East. Individually, none of these men had the personal color of Houston and Wallace, but the public ignored the facts when it thought of them. In its imagination, Jack Hays, the first captain of the Texas Rangers, was "a rough, bold giant, bewhiskered like a brigand, and wielding the strength of Hercules." Actually, though he led a band of tall, big-boned, and brawny-armed men, Hays himself was slim and slight-framed.[1] In build, Captain Ben McCulloch was "delicate,"[2] and Samuel Walker was, in size, undistinguished. Their reputation as giants was a product of the same popular fancy that made Daniel Boone "a mighty" hunter, even though he was actually slender and under six feet,[3] and Kit Carson a noble figure towering amid the silent wilderness,[4] despite the fact that he was not notably prepossessing. In the stories that circulate about them, remarkable fighters always sport remarkable physiques. The fabled feats of the Rangers helped build Texans, little and big, into awesome supermen.

American interest in these fellows was based largely upon the newspaper support—and notoriety—they received as fighters against Mexico. When a Major Norton, a Texan, went East in 1835, he received numerous testimonials of admiration and respect. The *Boston Times* exulted: "Who knows what embryo heroes this Texian war may not bring forth?"[5] When its editor thought of Major Norton, his heart leaped. Boston showered Norton with "a splendid rifle and equipments" and a large sum of money for Texan relief. Providence, Rhode Island, gave him a brace of pistols, and New York an "elegant sword" and the commission of colonel.[6] In Philadelphia, a crowd of several hundred persons eager for a glimpse of Samuel Walker, besieged his hotel. When he finally appeared, they saluted him with hearty cheers.[7] When Walker went on to New York to buy rifles and Colt's pistols, the *Spirit of the Times* hailed him as a leader of "the gallant Texas Rangers."[8] While recruiting Mexican War volunteers in Philadelphia, Captain Dan Drake Henrie drew high praise. A local newspaper described his escape from the Mexicans at Encarnacion as one of the most daring feats ever known—a true display of "the sterling qualities of the brave Texan Ranger."[9] The newspaper also considered Henrie "a bold, intelligent, and dashing officer," who would give his men every chance to win distinction for themselves and honor for their country.

The Mexican War first focused the public eye on the Texas Rangers. Occasional mention of them had circulated in the United States from their earliest organization in 1835. But it was not until Zachary Taylor, with some fears and trepidations, accepted several companies of Rangers into national service that Texans so identified began attracting steady attention in the American press. These were the men whom Whitman described in glowing terms:

> They were the glory of the race of rangers,
> Matchless with horse, rifle, song, supper, courtship,
> Large, turbulent, generous, handsome, proud, and affectionate,
> Bearded, sunburnt, drest in the free costume of hunters,
> Not a single one over thirty years of age.[10]

Frederick Law Olmsted, one of the many travelers to Texas who were glad to leave and go home, said the appeal of the Rangers throughout the United States, especially during the Mexican War, was due to their "wild life and exciting combats," which were as "romantic and attractive to young men as any crusade of old."[11] Olmsted declared that their rolls included then "the names of many men who would never be suspected now of rampant blood and deviltry."

Samuel Walker was one of the Rangers' greatest daredevils. His feat in carrying information from General Taylor to the beleaguered Fort Brown and back to Taylor at Point Isabel was one of the great news stories of the war. Because of this bit of heroism, the twenty-three-year-old Texan became nationally famous. And his repute carried the name of the Texas Rangers echoing across the nation.[12] A poem celebrating Walker's bravery said:

> For a braver, or a better, or a more chivalrous knight
> Never put his lance in rest in the days when might was right;
> And he had the fox's cunning, and the eagle's restless eye,
> With his courage, to see danger, and that danger to defy.[13]

In November, 1847, the *Spirit of the Times* described the melancholia which settled over New York when it learned of Walker's death. The gallant Texan's fame had extended over the whole country, and had reached foreign and remote lands. Walker was well known in New York, and, the *Spirit* said, he had many friends, some of whom had witnessed, and all of whom had warmly admired, his "daring and intrepidity." The paper was confident that his daring deeds, which had already become part of the nation's glory, would be "immortal in history and in song."

During the early months of the Mexican War when the biggest group of Rangers were active, American papers pictured them as the most mettlesome men then fighting. The press considered the Rangers good copy because they were determined fighters who usually got what they went after. They were also widely known as the most incorrigible and unconventional lot American military disciplinarians ever had to put up with. Their motley garb was enough to catch any editor's eye and to make any Mexican light out for cover. Though he thought they were all but indescribable, a front-line correspondent at Buena Vista tried to picture them for readers back home in Washington. Their clothes and equipment made them a sight to behold, for each man dressed according to his own personal whim. They wore rough, broad-brimmed white wool hats with fronts turned up; "red or fancy colored shirts; and trousers either of green, black, yellow or blue Mexican buckskin," or common American domestic. All this they topped off with a couple of five-shooters or six-shooters, a rifle slung on their saddles, and at least two bowie knives.[14] Some wag, finding the job of describing them too much for him, gave up and said the Ranger uniform amounted mostly to "a dirty shirt and a five-shooter."[15]

At Perote, under Jack Hays, the Rangers wore a prodigious assortment of long-tailed blue coats and bobtailed black ones, slouchy felt hats, dirty panamas, and black leather caps. They were mounted on horses of all shapes and sizes, from Texas ponies to thoroughbreds. The arms of each Ranger excited the admiration and wonder of all. Every man carried a rifle and four pistols, two old style single-shooters and two brand new six-shooters. The Rangers also carried short knives, hemp ropes, rawhide riatas, or hair lariats, and "anything else they could tie to their saddles."[16] Their long matted hair and full beards made some observers think Taylor had let a gang of cutthroats join his army. Samuel Reid, a Ranger who wrote a book about them, remembered that the first time he saw the Rangers he was sure he had never glimpsed a rougher looking set of fellows.

When the Rangers first arrived in the vicinity of Monterrey to join the regulars, the commanding officer of one of their regiments was uncertain about how to greet General Zachary Taylor. "I don't know what the devil we ought to do about it," he said, "but I reckon we'd better all draw up in a line, and when he comes give him three cheers."

When Old Rough and Ready arrived, each Ranger whipped off his hat and tossed it into the air or sent it sailing over the General's head. Each man, drawing his revolver, fired five rounds, whooped, halloed, yelled, and did whatever else he saw fit.[17]

These demonstrations splendidly prepared General Taylor for the later escapades of the men who understood only one fight order: "All ready, boys? Go ahead."[18]

The big news stories on the Rangers early in the Mexican War grew out of their riotous behavior at the Battle of Monterrey. Their wholesale mistreatment of the citizens of Monterrey went a good deal beyond "the laws of war," and Mexico has not forgotten it. T. B. Thorpe's account of the proceedings in *Our Army at Monterey* makes it easy to see why:

They moved up one or two streets under a galling fire, amidst which Col. Woods's voice was distinctly heard cheering on his men, bidding them remember the cruelties of Mier, Goliad, and the massacre of Fannin's men. The Texians sent up their war-whoop of defiance, and from that time fought like enraged tigers. Gen. Lamar, mounted upon his white steed, seemed to loom up like a commanding spirit among his men, as he led them on to the charge. It was a terrible sight, . . . the Texians, adopting their own mode of fighting, soon broke into the shut-up houses, scaled walls, and appeared on the housetops. Wherever a Mexican displayed himself, the deadly fire of the rifle brought him down. Thus wildly rushing on, they soon reached Gen. Quitman, when the fight became terrible in the extreme.

Down the streets, where poured an infilading fire, which the Texians had to cross, they would single out a house on the opposite side; a few of their number, armed with heavy axes, would concentratedly rush for the door, and at a united blow batter it down; then, into the opening thus made, would rush the remainder. All would thus again be safely housed, and thus protected they would soon level the sides of the buildings, and work towards the centre of the city. The barricades of solid masonry that crossed the streets were thus made useless, and the showers of balls that swept in a continued stream through them fell harmlessly against naked walls. The invading foe *was in the heart of the city*, gnawing out its vitals. The Mexican soldiers were terror-stricken; the sealed up domiciles of the city would suddenly open upon them, filled with the most deadly foes; the escopet gave way before the rifle, whose unerring aim dealt death on every side.[19] The sharp crack of the Texan rifles mingled with the horrified shrieks of the women.[20] Cheer after cheer was heard in proud and exulting defiance, as the Texians . . . gained the housetops by means of ladders, while they poured in a rain of bullets upon the enemy on the opposite houses. It was indeed a most strange and novel scene of warfare.[21]

The Texans were maddened with disappointment when they heard Taylor's order that, since the Mexican forces had capitulated, the fighting should cease and the enemy be allowed to leave Monterrey with his arms. The Rangers had been hoping for the chance to crush completely the army of General Ampudia, who was responsible for much of the Texans' suffering while they were his prisoners at Mier in 1842. After the Battle of Monterrey Taylor granted most of his Rangers immediate discharges, for Old Rough and Ready could not contemplate with equanimity "living in Mexico with one thousand idle Texas Rangers."[22]

Quoting "a friend from western Texas," the *Spirit of the Times* paid tribute to a small body of Texas Rangers who repulsed miraculously a heavy Mexican attack. To this paper, the Texans were indomitable, lighthearted, endowed with great capacities for endurance, and, incidentally, sworn to hate Indians and Mexicans. But other descriptions of the Rangers played up their enormous disregard for discipline. Speaking of Hays's Rangers in Mexico City, one army correspondent said that "a nobler set of fellows than these same Texan tatterdemalions never unsheathed a sword in their country's cause, or offered up their lives on their country's altar." Young and vigorous, kind, generous, and brave, they purposely dressed themselves in outlandish garb, to prove to the world at a glance that they were neither regulars nor common volunteers, but Texas Rangers—"as free and unrestrained as the air they breathe."[23] General Taylor and his West Point spit and polish boys threw up their hands in disgust.

Samuel C. Reid's *Scouting Expeditions of McCulloch's Texas Rangers* (1847) gave the period one of the best obtainable descriptions of Ranger character and adventures during the battles along the Rio Grande. In book form and in quotations in newspapers, magazines, and almanacs, it was the most widely read source of information about the Rangers. Quoting it in 1847, the *Spirit* praised Jack Hays: "Were an account of the Indian fights, skirmishes, and adventures of Col. Hays to be given to the world, it would fill a volume, and the work would be looked upon rather as the effusion of a fertile imagination," composed of legendary tales and the adventures of some fictitious knight-errant, than as the faithful account of the achievements of a living man.

The Rangers entering Mexico City with Hays enjoyed hugely the sensation their arrival created among the Mexicans. One of them, John S. Ford, boasted that the natives thronged the streets

TEXAN RANGERS AT THE BATTLE OF MONTERREY

Rough and Ready Almanac
(Philadelphia, 1848)

"... remember the cruelties of Mier, Goliad, and the massacre of Fannin's men."

CROCKETT SNOWBALLING THE MEXICAN SOLDIERS INTO THE RIVER

Davy Crockett's Almanack
(Nashville, 1837)

"... it war a tuff time in Tecksass then, but we stood up to our lick log till we licked the pesky Spanyards as clean as a barked hemlock."

CAPT. SAMUEL WALKER

Brother Jonathan's Almanac (Philadelphia, 1847)

"And he had the fox's cunning and the eagle's restless eye,
With his courage, to see danger, and that danger to defy."

along which the Rangers passed, for "the greatest curiosity prevailed to get sight at 'Los Diabolos Tejanos'—the Texas dev-
ils."[24] The Mexican attitude toward "Tejanos," especially the
Rangers, was well known in the States. In 1836 New Orleans
read how downhearted the defeated Mexican army beyond the
Colorado looked when followed by 1,800 Texans determined to
prevent their molesting property. "The Mexicans appeared to
wish themselves at home again, never more to meddle with
the brave Texans."[25] In 1847 French-speaking people in New
Orleans read in *Le Courier* of a grave error some Mexican bandits had made in ambushing three Rangers. It seems that the
Mexicans, hiding between Mier and Camargo with the intention
of robbing a merchant and his two companions, accidentally
attacked three Texas Rangers who were, by chance, passing the
spot. The error was fatal to the three bandits, who thus left the
road open for the merchant's party.

The Texan notoriety below the border was easy to explain.
Since at any distance into the interior the Rangers served primarily as scouts or as guards for supply trains, they often
traveled in small groups and reported to headquarters only at
intervals. Whether the Rangers were friendly or under arms,
all natives in any region where they rode were deathly afraid of
them. And it was well they should be, for the Rangers lost their
sense of humor, to put it mildly, whenever they saw a Mexican.
If one of the Texans ever "turned up missing," Mexican blood
flowed. When the Mexicans nearest the spot where he had disappeared could not account for him, every male Mexican on
the place was speedily done for, guilty or not.[26] When Hays and
his Rangers stormed into Mexico City, their bad name did as
much for their success as the guns they carried, for to the Mexicans they were a fearsome breed of fighters, "semi-civilized,
half-man, half-devil, with a slight mixture of the lion and snap-
ping turtle." They had a more holy horror of Texans than of
the evil one himself.[27]

The story has long been told of the reception of a Texan and
two ministers at the heavenly gates. Saint Peter deliberated long
over the credentials of the men of God but passed the Texan

without a word. When the preachers asked him why, Saint Peter
is said to have replied, "Why shouldn't I pass him first? Texans
have scared the Devil out of more people than you and all your
colleagues put together." Perhaps the Texan was a Ranger.

Until the Civil War there was no opportunity to rate the
Texan, as a fighting man, against enemies sprung from his own
racial and cultural background. Numerous wild reports, and
some not so wild, had circulated in the United States about the
absence of law in many parts of Texas. According to these reports, fisticuffs were almost incessant between the settlers. One
might well have concluded that Texans brawled because there
was not much else to do. But none of these accounts praised
their impressive fighting ability. Rather they condemned, more
often than not, the reigning chaos that let fighting go on. Most
of the reports featuring the battling Texans pictured them in
combat with their two foreign enemies, Indians and Mexicans.
Though nobody ever doubted that both of these knew how to
put up a good fight, both proved inferior to the Texans. Perhaps
the Mexicans lacked compelling incentive, or courage. Certainly the Indians were handicapped by inferior equipment.
Though in American newspapers the Ranger victories seemed
inspired, the triumphs of demigods, closer examination might
have revealed a significant imbalance between the two sides.

Nobody knows just how much the reputation of the Rangers
might have suffered if their adversaries had equaled them. In
any event, the Texans owed part of their good name as super-
fighting men to their splendid fortune in meeting enemies they
could whip. Just as the picture of the typical southerner included slaves in its background, the Rangers' portrait was
incomplete without conquered Indians and Mexicans.

In 1853 an officer of the Ohio Volunteers in the Mexican War,
whose name has not been preserved, extolled the character of
the Texas Ranger. "As a mounted soldier he has no counterpart in any age or country. Neither Cavalier nor Cossack, Mame-
luke nor Moss-trooper are like him; and yet," said the officer, "in
some respects, he resembles them all. Chivalrous, bold and im-
petuous in action, he is yet wary and calculating, always

impatient of restraint, and sometimes unscrupulous and unmerciful." Not in uniform and undrilled, the Ranger performed his active duties thoroughly, but with little regard to order or system. "He is," the Ohioan concluded, "an excellent rider and a *dead shot.*"[28]

Crack rider and sure shot, the Texan gained fame as a fighter because he bought and protected his country with blood. To a great degree, he was a heroic figure and highly admired because he fought enemies Americans hated—and because he won victories America wanted him to win. The rest of him was legend.

An early paper in Texas described one of the things about the Rangers that appealed to the public's imagination and made it think that fear was always at least a day's ride behind them. In a conflict that took place in the early days of the Republic between a few Texans and a large party of Comanches, a Ranger was seen careening boldly about the field on horseback, dashing now at one Indian, now at another, yelling and whooping, and pointing his gun right and left but never firing. When the Texans had finally gained the victory and the Indians had "vamoosed" after suffering a severe loss, the Texan commander asked the lone Ranger, "Billy, what in the d——l were you doing, cavorting around, kicking up such a big splurge, and never hurting anything?"

"I was just bluffing, captain,—that's all."

"Bluffing?"

"Yes, you see, my ammunition give out, and I know'd the blasted redskins would find it out cussed soon if I didn't keep up a d——l of a conbobberation. So I just run into every one of the blasted critters, and every time they see'd my five-shooter pointed at 'em, didn't they dodge under their horses' bellies and throw up their shields. And may be I wasn't out of that chap's way in no time. He'd a seen I was doing nothing worth bragging about and I'd have had an arrow into my gizzard in a jiffy. So I just bluffed 'em, captain."[29]

Today everybody thinks of the Texan as a horseman. The Texas cowboy is usually, and erroneously, given credit for this impression, and the modern Texas folk hero, Pecos Bill, is indeed a cowboy second to none. But the Ranger preceded the cowpuncher by many years as a representative Texan. Two implements of combat, indispensable to the Ranger, set him apart from all earlier frontiersmen. These were his horse and his revolver. In mounted melees with Indians, or charging on a Saturday night down the village street, shouting and firing both his pistols at the moon, the Ranger in action was the familiar "Kentuckian" in a new role.

It did not take America long, once the Texas Ranger became famous, to conceive of the Typical Texan as something apart from his western forebears. The tradition of the Rangers is one of the grand heritages of modern Texas. Fighting as a Ranger fought, the Typical Texan replaced the Kentuckian as the most colorful of western characters, and supplanted him as the representative of all the West. By the time he became famous as a character type, a new West had appeared on the American scene. He was, with the possible exception of the Mountain Man, the first character type belonging to that new region. For a century now Tex has epitomized the men and the spirit of America's last frontier.

CHAPTER SIX

The Sky's the Limit

THE Typical Texan grew up in the days when American humor was highly inflated. America was never overly sober, but it was only after about 1830 that a genuinely native flavor in America's laughter came to be recognized and recorded by humorous writers.[1] To be sure, the comic spirit in America did not hover about in limbo until the nation's writers got around to encouraging it. From the earliest years of colonial settlement, a leaven of humor in the American temperament buoyed up spirits that otherwise might have buckled under pioneer hardships. Even in Puritan New England laughter was only partially throttled. The rest of the country read with relish the jokebooks printed in England and widely quoted in American newspapers. Furthermore, the people laughed readily at themselves and welcomed anybody able to express humorously the bounding good spirits that then pervaded much of American life.

In the West, the frontier character and the "half-horse, half-alligator" brand of humor were familiar long before astute professional humorists put them into print. Virile behavior and a bragging manner, characteristic of any people during their heroic age, had been basic in the American personality from the first settling of the frontier. Where the bare necessities of life came hard, a man's physical abilities counted for almost everything. Superior fighting prowess was universally admired. The frontiersman who could hold his own against such usual adversaries as floods and storms, bears and Indians, was merely average. Only the man of extraordinary talents could call forth real admiration. Since backwoodsmen and other frontier people valued most their ability to use their rifles, their axes, and their bare fists in subduing the wilderness, the westerner based his ideas of personal worth mainly on the extent to which a man had mastered those techniques.

55

In reporting his achievements, real or potential, the frontiers-man characteristically exaggerated. Perhaps his tendency to dress up the truth was the natural product of a world that had recently cast off its bonds and old conventions and now delighted in a new freedom the race had not known for generations.[2] At all events, if he wanted his own back patted, the backwoodsman knew he had to come across with a good story, or his audience would promptly remember more pressing business. If he spoke of himself as a fighter, he knew that whatever it was that forced him to fight had to be, by the same token, extraordinary. Otherwise he had nothing new to say, and hence nothing worth listening to. Accustomed to seeing nature magnificent and boundless, and to witnessing the natural elements operating upon the mightiest scale, the frontiersman fell easily, perhaps often unintentionally, into habitual exaggeration.[3]

A conversation shouted at a hotel table in Victoria, Texas, was typical: "To be worse than I am," roared one Texan, "is what I call perfectly ridiculous. I am sometimes ashamed of myself; and to be so I must be bad indeed, but Bill is still worse, and this I call ridiculous." During the meal the bad man called out to another, "Don't be afraid, fool! I never killed a man half as white as you are."[4]

Like Davy Crockett, who came home one morning with "sunrise in my pocket," a frontier Texan meant he felt all right when he said he had "a pretty considerable of a jug full of sun this morning."[5] His country had the greatest rivers, the richest fields, the tallest forests, and the most plentiful game, and was the most rapidly prospering place on earth.[6] And relating himself subconsciously to the burgeoning world about him he spoke of himself, his exploits, and his powers as if he were of a chosen people.

Sometimes a well-turned understatement could prove as effective as pulling both triggers at once when a frontiersman wanted to put over a point. The Texas Rangers mastered this kind of brag. "We had a little shooting," one said, "and he lost." Another reported: "We were camped out on the Pecos. A norther came up, I pulled the cover off, and he froze."[7]

Among frontiersmen there were few subtleties. Since they were embroiled in a life "thick with serious purpose"[8] and filled with dangers on every hand, their humor had to be bold, and it had to be expressed in words appropriate to their physical vigor and bounding emotions. A. W. Arrington found that when the westerner was in one of his fits of boisterous glee, his fancy seemed to strip off all control and laugh at all limitation. He turned heaven and earth into ridicule—not bitter, but comic and heroic. He jested alike with things sacred and profane; he shook "the sides of the world with 'quips and cranks' and fun and frolic."[9] A subtle, restrained humor would have suited him no better than a coldly rational religion. Without the leisure time and intellectual climate necessary for punctilious speech the West produced a humor that had little in common with the sharper wit of cultured society. The American westerner thought "tall" and talked "tall." When it became necessary to toe the mark, his actions were right in line.

As the heroic symbol of all westerners, Davy Crockett was the best tall talker, bar none. In a country where children apparently learned to exaggerate as soon as they could talk, Crockett could lay it on thicker than anybody. His homeland and his natural abilities were his great inspirations. Exaggeration as an aspect of American humor had its great flowering in his spirited bombast.

Edward Smith, an English emigration enthusiast, on his trip through northeastern Texas in 1849 discovered that the people he talked with were uniformly prone to exaggeration. The Texans, Smith said, ignored "better" and had forgotten long ago the useless word "good." Everything in Texas was "best."[10]

Texan settlers from the earliest colonization were fond of throwing their chests out and bragging to the sky. When Mrs. Holley in her *Texas* praised the region's natural promise, she voiced an attitude common throughout the West, where the average man, believing his "own region to be the garden of the West," argued that the West was "the garden of the world."[11] Ordinarily a settler, when he moved to Texas, transferred his affections to his new country and thereafter bragged as lustily about its virtues as he once had done about those of the section he came from. The "Texas Brag" was thus the full flowering of the typical American conviction of local excellence.

Though the Texan exaggerated for the same reasons that inspired other men of the frontier, a special situation encouraged him to boast about the country he had forded rivers and trudged weary roads to reach. He early began bragging about Texas in self-defense. He was keenly aware of the "G. T. T." reputation his country had gained throughout America and the world at large, and he knew that many people scoffed at the idea of Texas' ever producing a decent civilization out of such tatterdemalion materials. Its widely discussed poor land, its diseases, its bad Indians, and its wild animals were enough to down all but the sturdiest sympathies. The settlers realized that many of their friends and relatives considered their move to Texas foolhardy, if not insane, and that it appeared to them about equal to suicide at the end of nowhere. A comment in 1840 ran: "We have often heard of Nowhere, and supposed it was somewhere in Texas."[12]

Such thinking, surely, figured in the history of the "Texas Brag." No wonder letters from early Texas settlers to potential emigrants in the United States painted a glowing picture. The letter-writers were out to persuade the conservative stay-at-homes to join them, and they tried to do this by counteracting the unfavorable reports which many non-Texans swallowed whole. A Texas paper, the *Galveston Texas Times,* played up the news that a Mr. Groce had recently brought into the editor's office two potatoes, one weighing eight pounds, the other seven.[13] The same motive prompted a Houston editor to report that corn could be planted in Milam and Robertson counties in holes made in the soil with a spiked log. The field would need cultivation with a hoe only once, and the farmer could expect a yield of at least forty bushels to the acre.[14] And the *Victoria Texian Advocate* reported for the same reason the news that a turnip had just been pulled measuring two feet, eight inches around.[15] Even if the tendency to exaggerate had not come along in the personal makeup of many settlers, they would naturally have tried to challenge, as convincingly as possible, the slurs cast so often upon their country and themselves. They fought with no holds barred to discredit such criticism. If honesty could do the trick, very well, they told the truth. When strictly accurate reporting got them nowhere, they made up whatever stories seemed called for. Big-Foot Wallace's experience with his doubting friends in Virginia convinced him forever that if he wanted to make his point he had better hitch up his britches and lie. Most Texans agreed with his principle. The "John D. Golly Whopper" grew well in Texas ever afterward.[16]

A poem making the oral rounds about 1885 summed up the attitude that had been riling Texans for nearly two generations. It was called "Hell in Texas."

> The Devil in Hell we're told was chained,
> And a thousand years he there remained.
> He did not complain and he did not groan,
> But determined he'd start a Hell of his own,
>
> Where he could torment the souls of men
> Without being chained in a prison pen.
> So he asked the Lord if he had on hand
> Anything left when he made this land.
>
> The Lord said "Yes, I had plenty on hand
> But I left it down on the Rio Grande.
> The fact is 'old boy'—the stuff is so poor
> You cannot use it in Hell any more."
>
> But the Devil went down and looked at the truck,
> Said even as a clear gift he was stuck,
> And after examining carefully well
> Pronounced it even too dry for a Hell —
>
> So, in order to get it off his hands,
> Lord promised the Devil to water the lands,
> For He had some water that was of no use —
> Was plumb cathartic and smelt like the deuce.
>
> So the trade was closed, the deed was given
> And the Lord went back to His home in Heaven —
> And the Devil had everything he needed
> To make a good Hell, and sure succeeded.

He fixed up thorns all over the trees,
And mixed the sand with millions of fleas;
Tarantulas scattered along the roads,
Put needles on cactus, horns on toads.

The rattlesnake bites and the scorpion stings,
The mosquito delights with its buzzing wings;
The sand burs prevail and so do the ants.
And those who sit down need soles on their pants.

The summer heat is a hundred and ten —
Too hot for the Devil, too hot for men;
The wild boar roams thru the black chapparell —
'Tis a hell of a place is the Texan Hell.[17]

The taunts of an easterner being driven over a barren stretch of western Texas were similar. When a gaudy bird new to the easterner flew up in front of him, the visitor asked what it was.

"That is a bird of paradise," said his Texan host.

The easterner rode on in silence for a while and then said: "Pretty long way from home, isn't he?"[18]

If the settler remembered the gibes showered upon him when he moved off to the wilderness, no one could expect him to admit, willingly, that he had been disappointed when he got there. If he dared mention hardships, he had to show that he had conquered them—or, at least, that something justified their cost. Otherwise he ran the risk of proving that the jeers he had once shrugged off as silly were, in fact, just and that his move and his judgment were faulty. The result was that from the start the Texan leaned over backward to emphasize his region's good points.

Then, too, some bragging Texans were perhaps motivated by the same feeling that leads a lonely man to whistle in the dark.[19] There is no doubt that western American humor resulted from an oversupply of frontier spirits. But it often served as a tonic to keep those spirits in the pink of condition. The "Texas Brag" emerged full-grown from the settler's own conviction that Texas deserved a lot of praise, as well as from his desire to prove to his friends back home that he had found what he had said he was going to. Hence he bragged, partly, to quiet his American critics.

But behind his exaggerations lay, at times, an unexpressed realization that the louder he boasted the happier his lot appeared.

In addition, the attitude of "foreigners," reading into the Texan character a bent for boasting because they imagined the Texan in the familiar western guise, may have suggested to him a role that, half-consciously, he began playing.

Whatever the cause or causes, Texas from its beginning has tickled the fancy of its people. Like any country which has had to bear verbal and physical attack, Texas elicited her citizens' enthusiastic devotion. Patriotism flourishes most heartily during periods of threat to the honor and survival of one's country, and early Texans had plenty of experience with both kinds of threat. During two wars, the Revolution and the Mexican War, and during unnumbered encounters with Indians and Mexican guerrillas, the Texans had to fight for their homeland. When such physical dangers were coupled with the vigorous disrespect of many outsiders for Texas and the Texans, the inevitable result was an ardent concern for Texas that has continued to burn in the hearts of her people.

People outside Texas early became aware of the "Texas Brag." In 1847 the *New York Spirit of the Times* printed "A Texas Snake Story" which described a snake in Texas with a girth as big as the belly of a horse. The paper admitted, in all fairness it said, that "Texas *is* a great country, but they have some very great liars there, for a new country."[20] In 1850, when a Texan told Matilda Houstoun, the English traveler, that he had seen a buffalo on the Texas prairie weighing two thousand stone, she remarked that though she had never heard of Texans' heads being submitted to the examination of a phrenologist, she imagined that "the bump of invention" would be found highly developed. Another Texan's report made her even more certain. This one swore that he had met a Comanche bringing home human legs and arms to cook for supper.[21] *The American Joe Miller* for 1840 quoted a Texan joke that ran like this: "A beet root is now exhibiting in Velasco, Texas, measuring thirty inches in length and forty-two in circumference. *Beat* this who can!"[22]

A Texan farmer and a man from Illinois were speaking of raising corn. To the Illinois man's boast of the superior yield of prairie land, the Texan replied: "I'll tell you what, stranger, they make large corn in your clearing, but it ain't a circumstance to what we raise on the Colorado bottoms. Why, the corn there averages thirty feet in height, with twelve ears to a stalk, and a gourd of shelled corn at the top!"[23] And the *Boston Flag of Our Union* said that a stalk of corn grew so high in Texas that the government bought it for a lighthouse.[24]

As early as 1830, the "Texas Brag" was finding its way into print. G. B. Cotten's *Texas Gazette* in San Felipe de Austin quoted a former Kentuckian who was sure he had done right to come to Texas. Drawing a deep breath, the newcomer proclaimed:

I can raise larger and better pork in Texas, than I could in Kentucky with all the corn I could give them! I can raise *ten calves* in Texas [with less effort] than I could *one* in Kentucky! ! I can kill a better and fatter beef among my stock, in the winter, than I ever saw butchered from the *stall* in Kentucky! ! ! I can raise horses in proportion to cattle! ! ! ! I can raise more corn to the acre that I could in Kentucky, and *with less* labor! ! ! ! ! My peas grow larger, and the hulls fill better *here* than I ever had them to in Kentucky! ! ! ! ! ! A volunteer plant of the *weed* (which is contraband here,) grew more luxuriantly in the back of my garden, last year, without being cultivated, than I ever had it do in Kentucky, with all the topping, suckering, worming, etc. that I could do to *it* there! ! ! ! ! ! ! Hemp I dare say would grow better here than in Kentucky, but I think, for cables or strong ropes, the *cabrista*, or rope made of the wild horse hair, preferable to those made of hemp! ! ! ! ! ! ! ! For comfortable and lasting apparel, give me the well dressed Texas buckskin in preference to all the ROTTED hemp, in Kentucky! ! ! ! ! ! ! ! ! My wife, Messrs. Editors, has not yet got *under way*, at gardening, but I pledge you my word I have never seen, in Kentucky, or elsewhere, as large, beautiful white cabbage as I saw in Mrs. ——'s garden in August. I was compelled to dine with her—I ate up the subject! ! ! ! ! ! ! ! ! ![25]

Another farmer bragged of his corn crop. "I have two fine boys who worked hard for this crop. I was in hopes when it was laid by, there'd be some rest for them." But, he said, shaking his head wistfully, "I reckon I was mistaken. When we send them for corn and I see them staggering under the weight of an ear, one at each end of it, I can't help but feel sorry for them."[26]

In Fayette County, a farmer was distressed because the ears of his corn grew so large that the stalks snapped off at the roots before the ears half matured. The farmer harvested his crop, but although the grains had shriveled up to half their original size, they were so big and so hard that his horses and cows could neither bite them nor swallow them whole, so he built a fence out of them. He said, "The fence is still standing, and bids fair to become *petrified* in the course of time."[27]

Another newspaper description sounds equally tall. A little town in Texas which had been overlooked by Dickens and other English travelers was, said the report, "all sorts of a stirring place." In one day recently they had had two street fights, hanged a man, ridden three men out of town on a rail, got up a quarter horse race, a turkey shooting, a gander pulling, a dog fight, a preaching by a circuit rider, who afterwards ran a foot race for apple jack all around, and, as if this was not enough, the judge of the court, after losing a year's salary at single-handed poker, and whipping a person who said he didn't understand the game, went out and helped lynch his grandfather for hog stealing.[28]

Texans were no slouches when it came to reporting their own abilities. A Texan scout whom Crockett met while on his way to San Antonio was perhaps typical. Crockett asked the "smart, active young fellow" about himself. The Texan said he was a whole menagerie. "I'm shaggy as a bear, wolfish about the head, active as a cougar, and can grin like a hyena until the bark will curl off a gum tree. There's a sprinkling of all sorts in me, from the lion down to the skunk; and before the war is over you'll pronounce me an entire Zoological Institute, or I miss a figure in my calculation." Throwing back his shoulders, the Texan vowed he could "swallow Santa Anna whole, if you will only skewer back his ears, and grease his head a little."[29]

Mrs. Holley's *Texas* is the earliest book praising the fertility of Texas soil. In the letters she wrote in 1831, she presented

"factual" information, though surely many readers recognized
it as first cousin to the tall-tale lore of the frontier. Mrs. Holley
said that Texas fields once planted in pumpkins seldom needed
planting a second time. An acre of sweet potatoes commonly
yielded five hundred bushels, some of the potatoes weighing
four to seven pounds. In such a marvelous country, it was a
task to find any shortcomings, but Mrs. Holley had to admit
one. Good as everything else about Texas was, cooks did not
grow on the Texas trees.[30]

Hell in Texas? If Hell was like this Texas, few Texans saw
any reason to behave.

CHAPTER SEVEN

Strangers on the Place

A RMCHAIR tourists have long been among booksellers' best customers. Certainly they comprised a good market during the decades when the American West was open for settlement. Travelers, well aware of this public's eagerness for firsthand news of the West, published voluminous travel accounts to meet their enthusiasm. Through the years travel writers compiled a sizable shelf of books about Texas. Some of these volumes went through multiple editions, while for others a single small printing proved more than sufficient. Some were low-quality writing as well as reporting; others were the heady stuff out of which epics could be written. In nearly all of them there surged the early rawness, wildness, and unmistakable promise of new country.

The strangers who braved the rigors of travel and made their way to Texas were a conglomeration of all types. Some came determined to see only the worst, and were not disappointed. Others hoped to find merit, and did. Apparently nobody ever came to Texas and wrote about what he saw without expressing some pretty definite conclusions. Texas during the pioneer period simply was not a world that left its visitors unaffected. The serious historian is right to reject much of what he finds in these travelogues, for they almost never sound like reasoned verdicts; details in them differ too widely. And that is to be expected, because most of the travelers who ventured into print were anything but scholars and trained observers.

We know very little about most of the intrepid individuals who published books on their Texas travels. Like the people they described, they rose out of anonymity for a little while and soon sank back into it. Most of them are known today only through the wide-eyed volumes they wrote. The majority of the authors came from older sections of the United States, but an

65

important and highly articulate group came from Europe. Some were abolitionists determined to squelch every possible chance of Texas' ever becoming another slave state. Some belonged to the haughty school which marked Texas off flatly as "an Elysium of Rogues." Some thought that geographically Texas was hopeless and ought never to be allowed to become an economic burden on the American taxpayer. Some, especially the women, clutching their well-worn copies of Cooper and Sir Walter Scott, came looking for the derring-do heroes of romance, and they found them.

The modern reader may well be surprised that any of the sojourners returned home with favorable opinions of life in Texas. Travel to and in Texas before the Civil War was an ordeal. The roads were poor and the streams often hazardous, for there were few bridges and no systems of flood control. When asked how they came to Texas, by water or by land, travelers could often truly say, "By both—mud!" Public lodgings were scarce and in many sections nonexistent. Fortunately, a good deal of southern hospitality had filtered into Texas, so that it was usually easy to find free board and bed in a cabin or lean-to along the road. But it was not always safe to accept such hospitality, even when at sundown the host had greeted the strangers on the place with a "Howdy!" and a "Light and come on in."

In Texas, which in 1836 numbered only 30,000 people and ten years later could claim no more than 100,000, the towns were at best crude eruptions in the clearings and on the prairies, which to a city-bred American offered few of the comforts of home. To a European the settlements seemed even worse. The people in those towns and on the farms, in the forests and galloping across the buffalo and Indian country were like nothing most of the newcomers had ever seen. In the printed reports which the strangers circulated once they got back to civilization, the Texans are described as an essentially new race, promising to make their presence felt in any company. Sometimes the travelers had something new to say about the Texans; sometimes they simply echoed the notions of earlier commentators.

Sometimes they liked what they saw; sometimes the picture revolted them, as it perhaps naturally would since many of the writers came to Texas purely to observe, not to sympathize with and excuse what they found. The public which bought their books made up its mind about the Typical Texan on the basis of much that it read in them.

The travel accounts which affected the Texan Tradition most profoundly were authentic records of personal experience. Their authors had gone to Texas and had evaluated the country and its people for themselves. Their books are at least the sincere expression of what they considered true. A few writers, however, were fakes. They might or might not have set foot on Lone Star soil or even have seen a Texan. But this did not keep them from broadcasting their opinions, in the form of spurious travelogues, far and wide to an often gullible public. It was of such charlatans that Sam Slick complained: "I seldom or never talk to none o' them unless it be to bam 'em. They think they know everything, and all they got to do is, to up Hudson like a shot, into the lakes full split, off to Mississippi and down to New Orleans full chisel, back to New York and up Killock, and home in a liner, and write a book." Sam said (for his author, T. C. Haliburton) that their travel notes were all the same. "Spittin'— gougin', — lynchin', — burnin' alive, — steam-boats blowed up — snags, slavery, — stealin, — Texas, — state prisons, — men talk slow, — women talk loud, — both walk fast, — chat in steam-boats and stage-coaches, — anecdotes, and so on. Then out comes a book." Sam snorted that he "wouldn't give a chaw of tobackey for the books of all of 'em tied up and put into a meal-bag together."[1]

Fake or fact, the travel literature of early Texas stimulated the mind of the average reader. Then as now, he read less for facts than for support of his own opinions, which were often inaccurate notions deriving from such "authorities" as almanacs and jokebooks. To this undiscriminating reader, a mere suggestion that Texans were wild men was more acceptable than the duller declaration that Texans were ordinary human beings who knew society's rules and usually obeyed them. The effect of a travel book's description of Texans depended largely upon the prejudice of the reader. It was difficult, if not impossible, for the public to lay aside such notions as "slavery" and "rascality" and "badlands" when it read these chronicles, and thus the books were sometimes fodder for ridiculously biased opinions.

As a whole, these travelogues had as much appeal as fiction. Indeed, they thrilled many readers more because they reported actual adventures in a real world. Almost any one of these volumes written before Sumter furnished tasty reading about swashbuckling Texans fighting Mexicans, Indians, or each other. The empty country, be it Cross Timbers, Piney Woods, or Plains, was exciting to read about too.

On the question of Texan character the travelers split into two factions, with most of the voting going "anti." The unfavorable group seems to have lost what sense of humor it ever had when it came to evaluating Texans. One may well wonder what it was the visitors expected that was so much better than what they found. Clearly, few if any of them had personally experienced the trials of settling a wilderness. Had they been forced to "dig into" a new country with the aim of making a home in it, perhaps their opinions of the people so occupied would have been less critical. At all events, the fact that hardships and privations rarely bring out the most charming streaks in a man's nature seldom struck them as an excuse for the shortcomings of the settlers. Yet, while doubtless there was plenty of evil in evidence, this was just as surely not the full story.

These ill-tempered guests wholly supported the belief that Texas was a great "valley of rascals." The anti-Texas newspapers never pushed this idea more vigorously than did such writers as Charles Hooton and Captain Frederick Marryat. A. A. Parker wrote after his month's sojourn that in some ways Texas was preferable to New England. For example, in New England, one spent most of his energies in earning a living. "Here, at the north," Parker grumbled, "the great anxiety is, how we shall live—wherewithal shall we be clothed, and how we can turn a penny to 'get gain.'" But in Texas where life came easy, the people worried most about how to kill time. Whereas

New Englanders managed to live in spite of nature, nature made the Texans "live in spite of themselves."[2]

Parker was pleased enough at the fine climate and fertility of Texas, but he noted more than once that the Texans "strive hard not to live." His reference was of course to what struck him as the settlers' excessive taste for fighting. His allusions to their lack of discipline were not emphatic enough to have greatly influenced the spread of this aspect of the Texan Tradition, but they may easily have been among the suggestions which, working in imaginative minds, fathered the conception of the Texan as a super-fighting man. It would be interesting to know how much, if at all, Parker's version of Texan character warmed the imagination—or aroused the fears—of later travelers.

The Texans, good or bad, usually responded in kind to the way the stranger treated them. If the visitor expected them to be a barbarous lot, and if they got wind of it, he stood a splendid chance of finding them just that. If his questions suggested anything sneering or belittling, the answers were correspondingly hostile. For example, one Texan settler, resenting an arrogant question about the type of money used in Texas, replied: "We pay in cows for large sums, throw in the calves for change."[3] The frontiersman was ordinarily too straightforward in his dealings with strangers not to play up to them uncouthly when he figured they considered him uncouth to start with.[4]

Perhaps this explains some of the bad impression Charles Hooton took home to London after a year's stay on Galveston Island. Hooton's memories of his months in Texas were painful partly as the result of poor health and an uncomfortable climate; but his scorn for the people must surely have waved like a red flag before them, and they must have reacted to it in no friendly fashion.

Hooton was contemptuous enough of living conditions in Texas, but his acrimony became really inspired when he lit into the people themselves. "Scoundrelism," he cried, "constitutes the larger portion of the present population of Texas."[5] To Hooton, "Dog-law" and common law in Texas were about the same thing. Throughout the country, knives, pistols, and rifles

had the last say in any personal "difficulty."[6] It was so common
for men to carry bowie knives between their shoulder blades
that it meant war if, during arguments, either party attempted
to scratch the back of his head. Travel, unless elaborately
planned, was perilous: if one wanted to be safe in Texas he
should journey only as a member of a big party, "well armed,
accoutred, and provisioned."[7] The danger lay not in Indians and
the usual hazards of the frontier, said Hooton, but in the Texans
themselves.

Colonel Edward Stiff was one of the many travelers who
came to Texas "well armed and accoutred." The fact that trouble
bypassed him surprised him so that he published a guess as to
the reason. Throughout all his travels in Texas, he said, he never
was once assaulted. His good fortune was due, he felt, to his
complete equipment for defense and his determination to move
on in the even tenor of his way and to "send to eternity" the
first person who sought his life.[8]

Stiff had reason to expect hostility from some of the men he
met on the road or in the inns where he sometimes spent the
night. One evening Stiff learned that eight of the fourteen other
guests at a tavern were confessed murderers. The first, a tall,
red-whiskered, villainous-looking man, had killed a "damned
rascal in Kentucky," was glad of it, and threatened the same
end to any person who even resembled his victim. The second,
a Creole "bloated by brandy," swore that liquor was the only
god. The third, a refugee from Canadian justice, had killed his
sweetheart and her father when the latter blocked their marriage. The fourth had robbed an eastern capitalist. The fifth and
sixth had got their victims in a drunken brawl and a duel. The
seventh had shot a judge for jailing him unjustly. The eighth
had murdered a witness who had testified against him in court,
and he declared vehemently that if there "had been no such
place as Texas, I would have been hanged." Of the other six
lodgers, four had absconded for debt, one was a rapist, and one
had fled on a charge of fraudulent insolvency and swindling.

Colonel Stiff was once attending a Houston theater when
Big Sam himself showed up for the performance. As the or-

chestra was discoursing sweetly, three cheers proclaimed the arrival of the President of Texas. This outburst was speedily followed by hissing, pistol shots, and the glistening of bowie knives. Many men in the audience joined in with volleys of profanity, some leveled at the President, some at the mayor, some at the police. With relief Stiff reported that "when at length all seemed exhausted, the field of battle was examined and three reported wounded; killed none."[9]

Another Texan whom Stiff described could well be a character in any of today's western movies. As the guest at a tavern dance, Stiff sat on the side lines well out of danger. One of the late arrivals to the party impressed the traveler especially. The Texan was dressed in a suit of buckskin that fitted his frame almost as closely as his own hide. Around his waist he wore a brace of pistols and a knife with a gleaming twelve-inch blade, and he carried in one hand a rifle of splendid workmanship. Entering the room, the man glanced carefully about. Then, satisfied that he could expect no special trouble, he placed the rifle on a convenient rack and joined the dancing.[10]

Stiff may or may not have told the truth; certainly his Texans sound like the figments of a vigorous imagination. But such people as the many roisterous fellows in his book probably seemed believable enough to a large group of American readers who had numerous occasions to read of Texans just as startling as these.

During his horseback trip in 1841 from St. Louis, the Reverend T. A. Morris, a delegate from Ohio to a Methodist meeting in Texas, met a Texan armed with a weapon different from any Morris had ever seen. It was a pistol and a bowie knife made in one solid piece, with the back of the knife welded to the under side of the barrel, and the blade projecting several inches beyond. Morris regretted that public sentiment tolerated the savage practice of carrying such frightful instruments as this, as well as ordinary pistols, dirks, and bowie knives.[11] Though he suffered no actual harm from personal contact with the Texans, he never at any time relaxed in Texas and his nerves always stayed at least two jumps ahead of him.

Nor did Frederick Law Olmsted's composure fare much better. Olmsted traveled in Texas primarily to observe slavery. His dislike of the Texans was based largely on his disgust at their owning slaves. And he considered the Texans little worse than any other people in slave territory, except for the fact that they always went armed. Olmsted found that Colt's six-shooters were standard equipment for every Texan. Olmsted was alarmed at learning that "there are probably in Texas about as many revolvers as male adults,"[12] but the femininity of the women pleased him very much. Though he never stated specifically what he meant by his term, "true Texan," the answer becomes an easy guess when he says that the women of East Texas, whether mistresses of slaves or only of their own frying pan, had "the tender hearts and some of the gentle delicacy that your 'true Texan' lacks."[13] Apparently, Olmsted saw on his journey no tender, gentle-hearted Texans. In that, he was not alone.

Among the travel writers who reviled the Texans, Captain Frederick Marryat, the popular British author, leads the field. Hooton and the others spoke from personal experience, but Marryat's book is one of the strangest, one of the most vitriolic fabrications that ever found its way into print.

Marryat's odd volume belongs as logically to fiction as it does to travel literature. But at the time of its appearance, few if any readers considered it a novel. Most took it as fact. On the surface, *The Travels and Adventures of Monsieur Violet in California, Sonora, and Western Texas* (1843) looks like authentic travel experience. The majority of its details ring so true that it could easily convince unskeptical readers. Nevertheless, statements like the following no doubt raised some eyebrows: "The climate of the western coast of America is the finest in the world, with an air so pure, that during the intense heat of summer, a bullock, killed, cleansed, and cut into slices, will keep for months without any salting nor smoking."[14]

Since Marryat had never been to Texas, he drew upon the accounts of actual travelers for much of his information. If his debt to other authors had ended here, Marryat would have escaped most of the wrath that fell on him. His big mistake was in presenting, as his own, great blocks of material lifted bodily from two of the most widely read works of the period, Kendall's *Narrative of the Texan Santa Fe Expedition* (1844) and Josiah Gregg's *Commerce of the Prairies* (1844), both of which had appeared before 1843 as newspaper serials. Both authors shortly discovered Marryat's plagiarism and were quick to object. Nevertheless his book enjoyed a commercial success, even though it is reasonable enough to surmise, as one critic has done, that "so chaotic and wearisome a production can hardly have commanded a very wide circle of readers of any age."[15] The fact is that it appeared in at least ten editions, both English and American, in the first sixty years after its first publication.

Throughout the pages devoted to M. Violet's travels in Texas, the writer's sympathy lies wholly with the Indians and the Mexicans. The Texas settlers are all squatters, interlopers on land to which they have no claim. Marryat declares that "expansionists" colonized Texas, determined to create from it two or three new slave states. But Marryat's resentment of the Texans is not clearly due to their owning slaves, as Benjamin Lundy's had been in his two pamphlets, *The War in Texas* (1837) and *The Origin and True Cause of the Texan Insurrection*. Though it seems unlikely that many American readers could ever have taken Marryat's Texans seriously, his book is the most caustic treatment of Texan character ever published, and no one could possibly like the Lone Star men better for having read it.

M. Violet carefully avoided associating with the Texans. "Indeed," he says, "we had no contact whatever with them, except that one day Roche thrashed two of them with his shillalah for ill-treating an old Indian."[16] He did, at a distance, form a long list of opinions about them—all bad. The future of Texas seemed dark indeed because her citizens were so "utterly depraved." The only two Texans whom Violet respected, Stephen F. Austin and Sam Houston, decided, according to Marryat, to quit the country in disgust at its demoralized condition. Numerous bands of robbers continually preyed upon travelers, attacking and plundering homes, violating women, and murdering at will. To get away with such crimes, these miscreants dressed and painted themselves as Indians. "Of course, what I have now stated, although well known to be a fact, is not likely to be mentioned in the Texan newspapers."[17]

Violet developed a special hatred for public officials in Texas. In Austin he saw them under "their true colors." Every evening, about five o'clock, almost all of them—including the President of the republic, the secretaries, judges, ministers, and members of Congress—were more or less tipsy. In the quarrels which ensued never a night passed without four or five stabbings or shootings. If the Texans were in their usual form, the riot continued during the major portion of the night.[18] Drunkenness and carousing were not their worst vices. Violet found that the Texans, everywhere, were inhospitable. Before Violet left San Antonio for Austin, a friend pressed five hundred dollars upon him with the warning that no Texan would ever give him even a tumbler of water unless he paid for it. Sure enough, near Austin, a bucket of water for his horses cost him a quarter. The friend cautioned him, too, that a visitor who passed even a few days among "the gallant members of Congress" should not be surprised if he missed his holsters, his stirrups, his blankets, or even one of his horses. Violet cut short his stay in Austin accordingly.

The presence of law courts in Texas, Violet said, did not prove that her citizens were law-abiding. Court days were the occasion for settlers from great distances to congregate, not because they were interested in the legalities, but because of the fine chance "to swap, to cheat, to gamble, and to pick pockets and quarrel."[19] And all this, Violet was sorry to say, took place in a country where at least ten thousand attorneys had settled. He reported that the President, the secretaries, the constables, tavern-keepers, generals, privates, sailors, porters, and horse-thieves were all originally lawyers.[20] Everyone else was a vagabond or scoundrel who had known better than to stay in the United States. On this account, Marryat rated the Texan character "wholly destitute of principle and probity." In his opinion, Texas was the "Alsatia of the United States."[21]

We have no way of knowing how M. Violet affected the Texans he scorned, but the chances are good that they considered his name appropriate.

There were travelers to Texas, unlike Marryat's Violet and Charles Hooton, who felt that the Texans' boisterous deportment might well spring from a natural surge of frontier spirits. These writers emphasized the solid, respectable qualities in the Texan that contributed, when properly corralled, to his effectiveness as a settler in a wilderness. More than one newcomer deeply admired the rugged, half-civilized adventurers intent upon carrying American supremacy to the Rio Grande. "Foreigners" familiar with the nature of western humor easily understood the Texan's swagger and gusto. Though literalists shuddered at many of the settlers' verbal expressions, those visitors willing to look for figurative meanings accepted the exuberance in Texan character as basically humorous and proof of good will.

Such a reporter was Mrs. Viele, the observant wife of an army officer stationed at Ringgold Barracks, Texas. In 1858 she published her account of time spent among the "gallant Texans." Her short residence in Texas was, to her, a romantic interlude among people who turned out to be a good deal more pleasant company than she had anticipated. Mrs. Viele was naïve, surely, in whitewashing the Texans completely. Apparently the men she met as a sheltered army wife always put on their best behavior around her. Reading her *Following the Drum": a Glimpse of Frontier Life,* one can today almost see the expectancy written on the faces of her many feminine readers as they rode with her, in fancy, through the wild, romantic West. As a glamorizer of Texan character, Mrs. Viele's book had no equal.

The Texans got off to a good start with the gentle Mrs. Viele when, on her arrival, one helped her from her boat to dry land. The water's shallowness kept the vessel from getting any closer to the shore than about twenty yards. To Mrs. Viele's amazement and delight, she found herself borne aloft like a baby in the arms of a "great stalwart Texan," who waded with her through the water until she reached firm footing.[22]

On her return east she happily told her readers: "I had once doubted the existence of those mythical beings called 'nature's noblemen,' but my stay in Texas relieved my mind from all uncertainty on the subject, for I found no lack of polish and courtesy, although the country is so newly settled."[23]

Dr. F. B. Page was another tourist on horseback who liked what he saw. Page realized that Texas, like any other frontier area, had its share of unprincipled men. He judged, however, that they were only a drop in the bucket compared "with the mighty mass of good principles, high virtues, and noble endeavors, that are found there."[24]

Nobody's enthusiasm for Texas surpassed that of Mrs. Mary Austin Holley. Mrs. Holley was a cousin of Stephen F. Austin, who as a Texas impresario stood to profit from her encouragement of colonization in his territory. Undoubtedly, she had one eye on his best interests when she published in 1833 *Texas; Observations, Historical, Geographical and Descriptive in a Series of Letters,* which held out to "persuadable" Americans the opportunities awaiting them in Texas if they would simply load up their belongings and go. She talked not only about miraculous sweet potato crops but also about the many upright, noble home builders who had made their homes and were seeking their fortunes in the new land.

"Milam," the pen name of one Henry Thompson of the *Philadelphia Herald and Sentinel,* praised the virtues of the Texan character. Angrily he rejected the charge that riffraff had forever ruined Texas for respectable colonization. "Does it injure the *marble,* for an immoral man to wash in a bathtub; or does a dwelling house depreciate in value from the accidental occupancy of a worthless tenant?"[25] "Milam" saw no evidence that Texas had suffered any permanent damage. In fact, in a land where one traveler insisted that the Irish potato when grown in Texas "becomes sweet, like the Southern or Carolina potatoe,"[26] there seemed to be no limit to Texas' great possibilities as a producer either of crops or of decent people.

Matilda Houstoun's *Texas and the Gulf of Mexico* agreed. The preparation Mrs. Houstoun had received before she came to Texas is obvious: "If we are to believe many of the writers of the day, murderers are to be met at every town, life is not safe for a moment, and private property is never respected. The whole of the population are described as dishonest and blood-thirsty; the very refuse of the vile."[27] Until she saw for herself, she believed that such reports were true. She noted that almost without exception the Texans carried "their national weapon, the bowie knife, about them, and this alone, one would imagine, would lead to a frequency of assassinations,"[28] since even at home in England, she recalled, when people had knives in their pockets they could hardly resist using them when angry, "and this in a country where punishment is sure to follow."

Mrs. Houstoun's later volume, *Hesperos: or, Travels in the West* (1850), mentions Shadowan, a notorious backwoods character, who was said to murder all travelers who put up at his place for the night. The writer never met this Shadowan personally, and was profoundly glad of it. She put him into her book only because he was one of the many exciting personalities she heard about on her western travels. No doubt she realized that he was exactly the kind of rough customer her readers expected her to meet. Mrs. Houstoun spoke up in defense of the forbidding looks of the Texans she encountered. She admitted that strangers had every reason to come to the worst possible conclusions about their character from the way they dressed. One could hardly imagine anything but bloodshed and strife when Texans insisted on "covering" themselves with pistols and bowie knives. But in spite of their frightening appearance, Mrs. Houstoun came to believe the Texans' own assurances that they really were as meek and gentle as lambs, and got themselves up in such fierce garbs only because it was "the prevailing fashion."[29]

These favorably inclined travelers declared that Texan character unquestionably included honesty and industry. J. O. Andrew, a preacher traveling in Texas, rejoiced in 1843 that Texas had outlived its former bad-boy stage and was now ready to behave itself. He met everywhere a warmhearted hospitality;

only once did he have to pay for a night's lodging.[30] George
Bonnell branded as "groundless" the American impression that
travel in Texas always endangered one's neck. Life was so much
safer in Texas than non-Texans supposed it to be, Bonnell declared, that the traveler who arrived loaded down with pistols
and knives could expect to be laughed at.[31] The citizens of
Milam, Texas, told T. A. Morris that the gallows they had built
on the town square was mainly to remind bad people in the
United States that if they did not wish to be hanged, they had
better keep out of Texas.[32]

The "pro" group generally agreed that the shortcomings of
the new civilization in Texas were those characteristic of any
freshly settled territory. Since Texas was at least as nearly free
of faults as any frontier, only a few years need pass until it
would be worthy of membership in a peaceful world community. In his enthusiasm over the prospects, F. B. Page ventured the guess that when time had fashioned and fitted it
together, Texas—and the character of her citizens—would be
found without a rival in history.[33]

Two aspects of Texan character aroused the greatest interest in these favorably disposed travelers: chivalry and aggressiveness. Of course, the same behavior, through hostile eyes,
could alienate as many visitors as it won; what one visitor called
bravery, for example, might look like criminality to another.
But imaginative observers, especially women, circulated their
conviction that Texans, as a class, were among the most chivalrous of men. This chivalry was in large measure due to the ex-
alted position of the female sex on the frontier. If Texans respected the ladies to an unusual degree, it was easy to see why.
One young bachelor from New England, in a letter to relatives,
put it straight enough: "I am dying fast. The city is a desert. No
business, no amusements. I have seen but one handsome woman
here, and she wasn't pretty. I wish I could get a wife; try for me,
do—will allow you a commission. I haven't a single button on all
my shirts; plague on such a life, I say I must either marry or
hang—no alternative."[34] Another bachelor wrote home, asking

for books and garden seeds. But his strongest plea was for *"one wife for me,* handsome &c. Mother knows what will suit me."[35] Still another, James B. Ransom, sounded like a bachelor when he toasted Texas in 1839 as "the proper empire for women; for 'tis here that the breast of each one of our countrymen is a temple in which she is sacredly and sentimentally worshipped."[36] Some decades later a cowboy spoke for most of the Texas bachelors of the half-century before him when he said that if he ever did get married he wanted a woman "what's all over gol-durned fluffs."[37]

Settlers in Texas quickly acquired a chivalrous manner. During the first several decades of settlement men outnumbered women ten to one, and with such competition, no man belittled "lady" manners if he had to use them to get a wife. A. A. Parker said simply that if the value of an article is enhanced in proportion to its scarcity, it was more excusable to fight for a lady in Texas than anywhere else under the sun.[38] The travelers attested to the fact that in such situations Texans often fought as actively with their gentlemanly graces as they did with their guns. And whether the men were protecting the women from the wilds of the wilderness or were fending off rival suitors, the girls loved it.

And so did the women travelers. They decorated their writings liberally with such terms as "great stalwart Texan," "daredevil Texan," and "nature's nobleman." The charmed Mrs. Viele passed along the good word that Texan hearts beat in time to the call of friendship, and that in Texas respect for women seemed an innate principle.[39] She was delighted to see that napkins were provided at her Galveston hotel as a special compliment to the fair sex, who all over Texas were "regarded with great honor and consideration."[40] This same lady never saw a "wall-flower," an unknown shrub in Texas,[41] because the men had too much gallantry to allow them to exist. Cora Montgomery, who was at Eagle Pass in 1852, said the Texans were "southern gentlemen" whose genteel behavior shamed the "chivalry of the knightly ages."[42] These women had, no doubt, cut

their literary teeth on *Ivanhoe* and *Marmion,* and never until
they came to Texas had they dreamed of *seeing* such figures.
In Texas their girlhood dreams came true.

The founder of Rio Grande City, Texas, Clay Davis, was Mrs.
Viele's idea of a "true specimen of the Texan." He was tall and
athletic, yet his delicately cut features, his carefully trimmed
mustache, and his air "bespoke rather the modern carpet knight
than the hero and pioneer of the wilderness."[43] She supposed it
was his association with the Mexicans that had given him this
mixture of western frankness and Spanish stateliness. Wherever
he got it, it certainly made him exciting to behold.

Aggressiveness was a trait most travelers found plentiful in
the Texans. Obviously, few people dared move to Texas in the
first place if they were not fairly well supplied with "push," for
they knew the frontier required it. Once they arrived, their basic
initiative kept them hustling. All travelers observed among the
people a perpetual dissatisfaction with the way things stood;
their determination to make things better appeared to be almost
a regional obsession. Danger and discomfort, as well as unlimited opportunities, fostered the "go-ahead" spirit that fired
the efforts of settlers throughout the West. Travelers did not
overlook the tremendous incentives to personal initiative that
vast, undeveloped Texas afforded. William Kennedy doubted
that in any part of the world was there a race of men "more
enterprising and energetic."[44] Like many observers, Kennedy
found the Texans superabundantly eager for action.

Many travelers declared, reasonably, that this enthusiasm
did not always lead the Texans into the worthiest pursuits.
Others argued that decency motivated them always. To the
latter, the courageous performance of the Texans as fighters in
the Revolution was the soundest possible evidence against the
charge that all Texans were criminals.

And so the argument ran on. A person who tried to believe
everything the travelers to Texas said must sooner or later have
given up in despair of ever learning the truth about the Texans.
What could one believe when the people who ought to know,

the ones who had gone to Texas to see for themselves, came home with such divergent reports? Were the Texans as depraved as Hooton insisted they were? Were they as noble as Mrs. Viele claimed? Or were they really in between, neither Prince Charmings nor hellions, but average men with a normal supply of all the human faults and virtues? The travelogues were not much help to an answer. You took your pick of what seemed most probable.

If you came, in time, to believe in the Typical Texan, you accepted the ladies' verdict that Texans were chivalrous, you took the word of Mrs. Holley and Parker that Texans were prone to brag, and you agreed with every traveler that Texans welcomed a fight and stayed in it till the other fellow gave up, bit the dust, or ran.

CHAPTER EIGHT

Fighters in the Spotlight

WHAT people heard about fighting in Texas was common currency of the dramatic stage. The American theater of the nineteenth century was in important ways like a newsreel. In the days before tabloid newspapers, picture magazines, and television, the public would have starved for much of the dramatic intensity of the news if the stage had not come to its relief. Throughout the years when any word from Texas was news, the theater did its utmost to capitalize on the situation. The most exciting brushes Americans had with Texans before the Civil War often came from the grease-painted and costumed "Texans" they saw on the boards.

Today one can only hazard a guess as to the nature of many of the earliest plays portraying life in Texas, for they have not survived. On the stage, setting for the most ephemeral of all the arts, a bad play is the most ephemeral work imaginable. Most of the Texas plays were bad. If all of them were not worthless, the exceptions have, in almost every case, disappeared for other reasons. Copyright laws that really protected an author's rights followed long after the period when Texas figured most prominently in the nation's drama. Few writers willingly saw their plays reduced to print, for this removed whatever hold the playwright had ever had on them. They became any actor's "property" then, and he could act them at will, with no fears of any legal opposition. Obviously, it behooved no writer to put his works into a form which an unauthorized party could lay hand on. So the printer and the playwright seldom met.

Of course, a company could not act without having its "prompter" copies, but in the case of most of the plays dealing with Texans, not even those lines have survived. Flimsy wooden theaters of the period had a way of burning down, taking with them into limbo costumes and fixtures, sometimes audiences and the texts of plays. No doubt some of the stage pieces in which Davy Crockett and Jack Long and the Rangers cavorted lay around in the bottom of some actor's trunk long after the stage had forgotten them. Those are the copies we wish we now had. But that "literature" has gone the way of all second-rate art. Today we can only make theories about why it ever appealed, or what it offered to the nourishment of the Typical Texan tradition.

Though we cannot read the plays themselves, advertisements and critical reviews, diaries and biographies afford some specific insights into many of the dramas that obviously dealt with Texan character. Even where we lack information about the plots and staging, conjecture is often easy about the treatment given the Texans, simply from drawing on the known facts of contemporary taste and acting technique. When Texas was attracting settlers and fighting its wars with Indians and Mexicans, the American stage was the happy home of melodrama. Except for the tried-and-true British classics, Americans had relatively little opportunity to see high quality plays. There was little serious domestic writing for the stage; what writing was done for it —except by such talented artists as Robert Montgomery Bird and George Henry Boker—played into the hands of actors who liked to throw themselves around in a good "show." The favored acting technique emphasized mobility, big gestures, and gallery-filling oratory. The greater the spectacle on the stage, the better all parties liked it. Texas was a natural subject for such extravagant stage treatment.

Stage managers without benefit of noticeable imagination frequently put together pieces based on big news stories, which they ornamented with subplots requiring bright costumes, maidens in great distress, and novel stage accessories. Such programs appealed for a night or two, or a week, and then were discarded, their length of run depending on the degree of interest that the news stories themselves possessed. The manager was lucky if he contrived to put his show on the stage before the public's concern with the subject died. If he failed to do so, he was often more prudent to call on a company of jugglers or well-trained dogs, for he knew as well as anyone that his "occasion" pieces were pretty weak stuff without the support of the public hunger for news behind them.

The Texas Revolution, Annexation, and the Mexican War were the three most active periods for stage Texans. Without the wars to spotlight them, plays about Texans would have been few, for the stage-pieces were rare which pictured Texans in any other role than that of American patriots fighting Mexico. Points as scattered as Cincinnati, St. Louis, New Orleans, and Portland, Maine, occasionally saw Texas plays. But just as most of the printed treatments of Texans were brought out by publishers in Philadelphia and New York, so theater audiences in these two cities witnessed most of the Texas plays.

One of the most successful of all the plays featuring Texans was *The Lone Star, or the Texan Bravo,* which Philadelphians applauded on August 15, 1853. The critics unanimously gave it the accolade, one of them declaring it the best "national piece" he had seen, another praising its subject as one filled with interest, a band of brave men struggling for freedom.[1] This play was a dramatization of a short novel of the same title by John Hovey Robinson.[2]

The story concerns the loves and escapades of Walter Ethington, an adventurer from Louisiana, known to the Mexicans as the Texan Bravo, and Captain Wilson, Texan Ranger and native of Kentucky. The time is the spring and summer following the death of Travis and Crockett in the Alamo. The plot is a loose thread linking the many skirmishes between the Rangers and Mexican guerrillas still fighting in Texas. Believing his bride-to-be had been untrue to him, Ethington had come to Texas to forget her and had found abundant adventure as a survivor of the Alamo. Carrying news of the Alamo defeat to Sam Houston, Ethington meets Captain Wilson, who asks him, "Stranger, have you been long in these diggins?"

"Several months," Ethington replies.

"Been in any fights?"

"A few."

"Can you stand fire?"

"A little."

"Cut off a sparrow's head at three hundred yards with a rifle?"

Ethington answers, "Never tried."

"I have," says Wilson, "and can do it. I'm a whole team and a dog under the wagon. Did you ever hear of the Texan Rangers?"

"Often, sir."

"They are perfect hosses, stranger, and I'm the alligator as commands 'em." Brandishing his rifle, Captain Wilson asks, "Do you see this hollow piece of steel? It carries ten balls to the pound, and is sartain death."

Wilson's great compliment to any man is: "I have heard about your fightin' and they say there is a great deal of the wild hoss in you, with a small sprinklin' of the Kentucky alligator and snappin' turtle." His pride in his newly adopted country is firmly rooted. He is convinced that it is "the 'tarnalest great Republic in the world." Captain Wilson, the Bravo, and other Texans fight all the Mexicans available, partly for the deliverance of Texas, but more for their love of "good hunting." During one of the combats a Texan named Ridgeley begins belaboring the Mexicans with a good-sized hunting ax. In his anger he shouts, "There's for the death of Travis, and Crockett, and Bowie!" Instantly the fighting ceases, and those of the enemy who can do so flee. Six are left behind, affording ample proof of the Texan's prowess.

Wilson's address to the Rangers before the San Jacinto fight reveals his pride in their reputation among the Mexicans. "Texans, hosses, and alligators from Old Kentucky!" he says happily,

Yonder are our enemies. You have got good rifles in your hands, and know how to use them. Don't fire until you are sure of your man, for we meet the foe one to three, and that's considerable odds, but do your duty, and we will whip them so they won't forget the Rangers while they remember anything of an airthly nature.

But Sam Houston, on the San Jacinto battlefield, voices the most memorable thought of the day. Pointing upward with his bloody sword, Captain Wilson draws Houston's attention to two enormous ravens poising above the scene of the conflict, their beaks turned toward the west. Several of the Rangers raise their guns to fire, but "Hold!" cries Houston. "The omen is a good one; it denotes the march of the empire westward!"

The earliest known play about Texans, *The Triumph of Texas, or, the Siege of San Antonio de Bexar*, greeted New York audiences on December 31, 1835, three years before the appearance of the first Texas novel, Anthony Ganilh's *Mexico Versus Texas*. The theater was packed, and receipts for the evening totaled the unusual sum of $1,700. A large crowd, unable to find seats elsewhere, sat on the stage, and hundreds were turned away at the box office. Since the text apparently disappeared with the public's interest in the subject, and since no critic printed his views of it, it is impossible to say definitely what impression this play sought to leave. Presumably it was favorable to the Texan cause at San Antonio, since a week later the same theater, the Bowery, sponsored a benefit "for the Texan patriots struggling for liberty." The *New York Times* carried a cast list, noting that one of the starring roles, played by an actor named St. Luke, was "Kentucky Harry." One is tempted to make more of this than the known facts indicate. But the appearance of a Kentucky character in a Texas play was one of the early links in the kinship of the Typical Texan to the famous Kentucky character type. In 1835, few Americans knew what kind of person the Texan would turn out to be; the author of this play was perhaps simply adopting a suggestion of the newspapers in making a Kentuckian the star. No other class of immigrants to Texas seemed more appropriate to furnish the stellar figure in the first dramatic treatment of the new men of the Southwest. Likely enough, "Kentucky Harry" in *The Triumph of Texas* expressed himself as Nimrod Wildfire, his fellow Kentuckian, had done in Paulding's play, *The Lion of the West*, five years earlier. Wildfire said he "hadn't found a fight for ten days and felt mighty wolfy about the head and shoulders."[3]

The next night, the American Theater in New Orleans gave a similar play, *The Fall of San Antonio, or Texas Victorious*. The critics ignored it, probably out of kindness, and it was quickly

forgotten. The playwright, N. H. Bannister, later became celebrated as a writer of action-packed dramas, the most noteworthy
being his *Putnam, the Iron Son of '76,* which in 1844 had an as-
tonishing run of seventy-eight nights in New York. This play,
ending with General Putnam's famous breakneck ride down
Horse Neck Hill, demonstrated Bannister's skill in filling the
stage with exciting spectacle. For many years it was revived an-
nually.[4] Bannister's *The Fall of San Antonio* was among the
first plays he wrote, if it was not the very first. It would be valuable to know how well developed his showmanship was at this
time, and especially to know what picture of the Texans he
gave. Certainly, if the play's title meant anything, he saw them
as good fighters.

On May 26, 1836, Philadelphians cheered *The Fall of the
Alamo, or, Texas and Her Oppressors,* a play rigged up to capitalize on the excitement created by the Alamo disaster and the
subsequent glorious victory at San Jacinto. For weeks the papers
were full of Texas news items, and many were as delighted at
Houston's victory as the *New York Herald,* which praised the
Texans whose "hearts were warmed with pure Anglo-Saxon
blood" and whose "spirit was unconquerable." The play itself
featured Crockett and William B. Travis, Santa Anna and General Cos. "Uncle Peleg Snow," a secondary character, was
spoken of in the advertisements as a "respectable old Yankee."
Did this perhaps serve notice that Peleg Snow was not a Yankee
peddler? This is the first mention of a Yankee in a Texas play.
Such a character in a stage-piece of this type was welcome because it gave eastern audiences the best possible chance to com-
pare Yankees to Texans. Nothing could emphasize their peculiar characteristics more colorfully than their joint appearance
on a stage. The Yankee's presence in this play was probably an
example of a common practice of contemporary stage managers,
who, regardless of logic, often worked "down-easters" into plays
simply because the character type was so popular. From the
dramatic standpoint, the appeal of the Yankee, and the Texan
too for that matter, was quite probably heightened when the

two personalities were brought into interplay before an audience. G. H. Hill, a favorite "Yankee" actor, played Uncle Peleg, thereby doubtless helping to sell the show to the public. Yet the action and noise of a Texas battle on the stage must have been a large factor in assuring the play's acceptance by an audience that liked lusty spectacles.

Santa Anna, or the Liberation of Texas played five performances to happy audiences at the Bowery Theater in New York. beginning June 20, 1836. The usual mixture of Mexican villains and Texas heroes crowded the stage. An actor named Cony played the part of Davy Crockett with the same gusto that had made him a favorite in earlier rip-snorting roles. The play attracted, every night, great crowds that shouted and roared when the Texans won.

Three years passed before the appearance of another noteworthy Texan play. With N. H. Bannister spotlighted as Crockett, an Alamo piece called *Crockett in Texas, or, the Massacre of the Alamo* occupied a New York theater's boards for a week in October, 1839. The drama had no special merit and appealed largely because it treated Crockett sympathetically and, even more, because it was packed with smoke and gunplay. For similar reasons, a play called *The Fall of the Alamo, or, the Death of Davy Crockett* succeeded in New Orleans during January, 1840.

The "G. T. T." talk found its way into the theater at least twice, once in 1839 when *Bennett in Texas* was given in New Orleans and again in 1844 when New York, Philadelphia, and London saw a highly successful farce, *G. T. T. Gone to Texas.* The New Orleans play was a fly-by-night effort from the pen, if not the brain, of Joseph M. Field, a popular contributor to the *Picayune* and the *New York Spirit of the Times.* William T. Porter, editor of the *Spirit,* wrote in 1845 that Field was "full of fun and frolic, and ready to go at anything in the ring—from pitch-and-toss to manslaughter;" but his play evidently lacked the pep of its author, for the papers quietly ignored it, except for an advertisement in the *Picayune* which read: "Mr. Bennett wishes it to be distinctly understood that his exile in Texas is entirely voluntary; solely induced by the faithlessness of the sex and the ingratitude of the government."[5] The play opened and closed the same night.

The other play, *G. T. T. Gone to Texas*, titillated audiences on both sides of the Atlantic for several months just prior to Texas' annexation. Founded on "the prevailing mania of bankrupts, swindlers, and thieves for emigrating to the land of the Lone Star,"[6] it was a spirited one-act comedy which chronicled the efforts of a Mr. Swellington to shrug off his debts by pretending to be absent in Texas. On the opening night in London, the play kept the audience in "the greatest merriment throughout," and Swellington announced that he would be "Gone to Texas" every night until further notice.[7]

Davy Crockett turned up again in Philadelphia in 1845 when a play featuring him, *The Lone Star, or Troubles in Texas*, ran at the Arch Street Theater. In addition to Davy, the cast included Mrs. Dickinson and Joel Bigelow, a Yankee. When the play was revived a year later, the famous Yankee comedian, J. S. Silsbee, played Bigelow. The Philadelphia critic, Charles Durang, dismissed this play as a "Yankee Western concoction of absurdity and modern stage humbug."[8] Apparently the less critical customers liked it well enough, for it played to five good houses.

The year 1846 saw the first in a long series of plays dramatizing the participation of Texans in the Mexican War. That play, *The Campaign on the Rio Grande, or Triumphs in Mexico*, was written immediately after its author, Walter M. Leman, received the news that hostilities had broken out on the Mexican border. General Taylor, Captain May, and Captain Walker, "a Texan Ranger," headed the cast. Since no description of the physiques or costumes specified for the actors has survived, it is impossible to know how the play influenced the idea that all Texans were big and brawny. Though Walker was actually small and slenderly made, with no remarkable or striking features, it is highly unlikely that this play so depicted him; for almost immediately after the news of Walker's bravery at Fort Brown reached the East, people there began conceiving of him as large, muscular, heavy-bearded, and fierce-looking.[9] Just as Walker's heroism was the first occasion for many non-Texans to hear about the Texas Rangers, so *The Campaign on the Rio Grande* was the first dramatic treatment of these colorful Texan fighters.[10]

The Battle of Texas brought Crockett and his Alamo colleagues back to a New York stage on December 29, 1846. Sam Houston and Thomas J. Rusk, then the United States senators from Texas, were visiting in New York when this play was performed. There is no record that they attended it, though it was noted that their arrival at the Bowery Circus the next evening brought forth a round of nine cheers from the audience. Their hosts may purposely have steered them away from the play, since one critic declared that the company at the Greenwich Theater, where *The Battle of Texas* was played, was so poorly balanced that its efforts were utterly wasted.[11] Another Mexican War play, *The Texan Rangers, or Elephant in Mexico*, was a New York hit in February, 1848, with Captain Walker as the featured character.

So much for the plays known today largely through hearsay and advertisements. A few others have survived either as the lines of actual plays, or in the story form on which the acting versions were based. One such is *Shot in the Eye, or, the Regulators of Texas*, which gave New Yorkers their first glimpse on the stage of the notorious society in the piney-woods section of Texas. Opening on September 3, 1849, it shared the billing at the Bowery with *Macbeth* for more than a week. This play, which was published as *Jack Long; or, the Shot in the Eye* by John Beer Johnstone,[12] was only one of several stage adaptations of Charles Wilkins Webber's long story, *Jack Long: or Shot in the Eye* (1846). It received more press notice than any previous Texan play. The *New York Sun* hailed its first performance with a warning to the public that it should secure its seats early, for the Bowery was sure to be crowded for many nights to come.

The drama painted a lurid picture, widely discussed in the papers from Maine to Louisiana, of the Regulators and Moderators war which had raged unchecked for years in Shelby

County, Texas. About his tale, Webber wrote: "If you have even a remote conception of the history of that republic and the general character of its social elements, you will be prepared for a good deal."[13] A resident of Shelby County reported in a letter to the *Portland* (Maine) *Daily American* that the citizens of the county were about equally divided into two groups. The Regulators, as one group was called, undertook to see that such individuals as were deemed undesirable should leave the community. The Moderators, declaring such doings to be illegal, determined to put a stop to the Regulators' high-handed activities. Within a few days from the time of the letter quoted in the Portland paper, the groups had fought two severe battles and many had been killed and wounded.[14]

The play's action springs from the refusal of Jack Long to join the Regulators because, as he says, "I don't train in that company." Hinch, the leader of the Regulators, and Long are rivals for the beautiful May Gibbs. Long is reminiscent of Cooper's stolid frontiersman, Natty Bumppo. Hinch, more cowardly than cunning, is the typical backwoods villain. The opening scene is laid in the street of a Texas village, where Hinch, intent on a plot to have Long accused of horse-stealing, meets his fellow Regulators, Stoner, Rees, and White. White, half drunk, curses Hinch for stealing a horse on his own hook without intending to share it with the group. Hinch admits his guilt, and White warns him that he must beware of Jack Long, the boldest man and the best shot in all Texas. While they are talking, Ben Small, an "original cute genius of a Yankee pedlar," enters and berates the Regulators for their misdeeds. A shot rings out, and Jack Long enters. He is the model frontiersman, both in looks and in equipment. He wears a hunter's garb of beaded buckskin, fringed with red and blue. In his belt he carries an Indian pipe, a tomahawk, an eight-inch bowie knife with buckhorn handle, a powder horn, and a shot pouch. His cap is made of squirrel skins with the trailing tails left on. His hair is long and his face bearded.

"Hullo," Long says. "What's Congress met for? Is there anything afoot that the Regulators are after so soon? What, President Hinch, is there a screw loose? Has the red nigger quit the chaparral to scare the pale-face; has the greasy red left his covert to bring blood and fire into the peaceful settlement? If 'tis so, Jack Long's head, hand and rifle are ready in the cause."

"The defenders of the settlement are sufficient," replies Hinch, "to meet the danger, should danger come."

"Oh, are they?" Jack counters. "Well, I am happy to hear it. You'll excuse me; but if anything of the sort happens, I mean to have a finger on the hair!" He flourishes his knife.

"You're no Regulator," Hinch retorts.

"Well, Regulator or no Regulator, I shall do it!"

"Then why not join us?"

"Because I don't like you," Long answers.

The Regulators exit muttering, leaving Long and the Yankee peddler talking. Presently, Jack excuses himself to escort May Gibbs to a shooting match. When Ben teases him, Jack replies, "Well! Where's the harm. 'Tisn't treason against the Lone Star State to love a pretty girl, is it? I think the best feather in a man's cap is the true affection of an honest-hearted maiden. Man's not a lonely animal. Woman was formed that he might love and honor her."

The next scene finds Bill Hinch at the Gibbs home, attempting to propose to May. She says that his hopes are idle. Hinch tells her that he knows she loves Jack Long, and he threatens Long's life. When Long enters, Hinch leaves in a rage. May's father readily consents to Jack's request for May's hand in marriage. The pleasant conversation is interrupted by a servant's cries that Gibbs's horse has been stolen.

The spotlight now moves to the shooting match, with a large party of settlers, the Regulators, and May and Jack on the stage. Merriment reigns until Hinch and Long take their places on the firing line. Hinch shoots and then turns to Jack. "Here, look! Look at that! Take a good look! Can you beat that?"

Jack laughs. "You don't call *that* shooting, do you?"

"I should like to see you beat it!"

"All right," says Jack, "set up that board and I'll put a bullet through the very hole you have made. It's a trick of mine—it's a way I larn't in old Kaintuck of always shooting the animal in the eye!" Then Long looks straight at Hinch. "If once I set eye to eye, my shot is always certain. I always hit him thar!"

As Long is shooting, Gibbs runs in to seek the aid of the Regulators in finding his horse. Some of the outlaws report that the animal has been found in Long's corral. This, of course, brings on a fight. Torn from his friends by the Regulators, Long is dragged out and severely whipped. When he returns, bound and bearing the scars of heavy punishment, Hinch laughs at him.

The peddler slips in and cuts Jack's fetters, and a Regulator shoots at Jack. He immediately fires back, sending his bullet through the outlaw's brain. Jack shouts to the Regulators: "One! In him behold the doom of all!"

And Stoner exclaims in awe, "Shot in the eye!"

Jack exits amid a volley of rifle fire.

In a gloomy swamp, Hinch, White, and Stoner, armed with rifles, lie in wait for Willy Jones, a peddler whom they intend to rob. They are desperate for enough money to quit the country, since they have been frightened by a mysterious killer who has shot four Regulators, all in the eye. The peddler enters, and they kill him.

At Ben's store, when a violent crash of thunder peals out, Ben tells May and her father that they must seek a place of safety. Jack Long, now partially crazed by his obsession for revenge, is visible momentarily in a flash of lightning. Long has not been seen in the settlement since the shooting match because, as Ben explains it, "he couldn't face the woman he loved arter the foul dishonor heaped upon him by that scoundrel Hinch." A shot is heard, and Stoner drags himself in, shot in the eye, and dies. In the distance, Long shouts: "Five! Five! Half my task is accomplished."

Alone in a log hut, Long broods over the wrongs done him. May enters and is attempting to soothe him when Hinch and White, at the window, try to shoot Long. When Long stirs, they withdraw quickly. Long goes to the window, fires, and kills White, then sets off in hot pursuit of Hinch. He trails him—

an incredible distance on foot—to the banks of the Rio Grande, where Hinch is trying to hail a boat when Long finds him. Hinch cries, "Mercy, mercy!"

Laughing derisively, Long shouts, "Mercy! Ha, ha, ha! seek it from the hungry lion, or the prowling tiger. What! Would you ask me to give up that which I have watched for and prayed for—the very life of my life's blood? The thought that has nourished me! The only draught of joy in my wrecked and blighted life! Ha, ha, ha! fool!"

Hinch hears May approaching in the underbrush and is overjoyed at the thought that she may be able to save his life. But just as May arrives to beg for Long's mercy, Jack shoots Hinch through the eye.

As the play ends, Long has regained his sanity, has married May, and has been cleared of the charges of stealing Gibbs's horse, but he is greatly troubled over the enormity of his revenge. To May he says, "Alas, I cannot clasp thee now. My hands are red with crime. The night of darkness has passed, and the day breaks! With sense comes sorrow. I am a blood-bespattered man! And I look but hopeless!"

Gibbs attempts to quiet his fears. "He who has sent affliction, will look with mercy on the deed done in your senses darkened. The reward of our State also awaits you."

And as May agrees, saying, "The deed will justify the means, and Heaven and man—," Long kneels with her and faces the audience to say, "I hope, will pardon Jack Long of Texas!"

The same actor who played Jack Long with great success next appeared in two Crockett plays, one in New York and the other in Philadelphia. H. E. Stevens seems to have had a special penchant for such parts, though none of the fugitive notices about his career make the reason clear. Was it temperament, build, or both that fitted him for Texan roles? Stevens had played Crockett in *The Lone Star, or Troubles in Texas* in Philadelphia in 1845. Now he appeared as Crockett in *The Lone Star* on October 25, 1849 in New York, and on August 30, 1850 as the same character in *The Texan Struggle*. The *Spirit of the*

Times was pleased with the play and reported that audiences would probably continue to be so for months to come.

Michael Bonham, or, the Fall of Bexar, by William Gilmore Simms, was the last on the list of pre-Civil War Texan plays.[15] Milledge L. Bonham, the Texas hero, was living in Charleston, South Carolina, at the time the Charleston Theater presented the play for two "more than creditable performances on 26 and 27 March 1855."[16] As Simms's biographer says, the play reads like "the work of a precocious youth of eighteen" rather than of a mature writer and student of the drama.[17] The principals in *Michael Bonham* are Colonel Milam, Bonham, Davy Crockett, two Mexican señoritas, and several Mexican officials of San Antonio. The action of this last play, like that of the earliest, dramatizes the Texans' capture of San Antonio, this time from Governor Esteban, father of Olivia, with whom Bonham had fallen in love after delivering her from Comanche kidnappers. The opening scene in the Texan camp finds the Texan fighters lolling about, some wearing hunting shirts, some buffalo and deer skins, all armed with bowie knives and rifles. Davy Crockett enters with a bear slung over his shoulder and announces that the last time he saw Bonham, the latter was just entering the gates of San Antonio disguised as a monk. They are discussing the wisdom of such a ruse when Bonham, now clad in the ornate costume of a Spanish Don, enters and proclaims: "It is ours, that brave old Spanish keep, with all its treasure, if we but battle as becomes a people, sprung from the Old Thirteen."

Crockett eagerly seconds Bonham's plan to return to San Antonio, again in disguise, to spy out the best mode of attack. He begs Bonham to let him go along:

You're a huckleberry above my persimmon. I can hunt and fight, I reckon, as well as any man. I can shake as clever a leg at a Virginny reel, when I'm a little up in sap, as any native this side of the etarnal ridge; and, though I say it myself, I have put up as decent a prayer as I have ever heard from any parson in all this nation of Texas, but that was when I was mightily scared, as I never expect to be scared again. But I can't do the many fine things you're up to. Yet, if there's anything that I *kin* do, say the word, and let me go with you.

Crockett promises to keep the secret, speak the truth, and stand by "with knife and rifle to the last beat of a big heart!"

Bonham assents. The signal for the attack will be a blast of their bugles from inside the walls of San Antonio.

Bonham, as a Don, and Crockett wearing the garb of a mule driver enter the city unmolested. They meet the governor, his daughter Olivia, and her cousin, Maria. The main talk they hear is of the masked ball to be given by the governor that evening. Bonham's manner immediately charms both Olivia and Maria. They know him only as Don Amador de Aguilar. The governor encourages Maria's interest in Bonham because he thinks she loves a Don Pedro, whom he dislikes intensely. Bonham and Crockett steal the keys to the city gates, and are confident of the success of their mission. The ball begins with Bonham wearing a monk's gown and Crockett—sworn to silence because he speaks no Spanish—disguised as a Comanche. Deeply infatuated with Bonham, Maria appears as an Aztec princess; and Olivia, who has learned of Maria's regard for Bonham, wears the habit of a nun.

The splendor of the scene dazzles Crockett, who whispers to Bonham:

Major, this is famous fine. My head is swimming fairly in the blaze of glory, jest as it used to swim when I looked on Old Hickory's. It's wonderful handsome. I never seed the thing better done at the White House.... Lord, what a shine of dresses. There's gold and silver enough about 'em to build a church, not leaving out the steeple. And look at the diamonds; I reckon, Major, them's the ra'al grit.

Plotting to kill his rival, Don Pedro learns that Amador is wearing the monk's garb. Bonham angers Maria by telling her he can never love her; Crockett stupidly speaks to her in English; and it is then that Maria's hatred for them both causes her to tell Don Pedro that Don Amador is actually the Texan rebel. The dramatic climax comes when the governor seeks to establish Bonham's true identity, without insulting him should his informer, Don Pedro, be mistaken.

The governor says: "Upon your arm, my father, you wear the holy symbol of your faith, but do you ever lift it to your lips?"

Bonham answers, "Behold!" and kisses the cross.

Aside to Don Pedro, Esteban whispers, "He could not do it better were he the archbishop of Mexico. Tell me that any heretic will kiss the Holy Cross. I know better." Then he continues, "Mark the further progress of my plan." Turning to Bonham, he says, "Hem! And now another question, Holy Father."

"It needs not, señor. I will spare you trouble, spare you some breath, and answer ere you ask me—I am suspected, first!"

"No, not exactly, but — "

" 'Tis so. I see it in the eyes of all, and hear it in your accents."

"Nay, good father!" says the governor, "You are too quick, but say that something of this sort is the difficulty, and you will at once see the propriety, and the prudence, and the necessity of accepting my protection! My officers, you perceive, are furious; it will not be possible to restrain them; they are terrible as lions in rage, and your only hope of safety is in — ... "

"There needs no parley, señors," Bonham declares, "your fierce warriors, are not so dreadful in mine eyes, to make me seek your protection. You would have my secret. 'Tis yours!" And throwing off his monk's disguise he shouts, "Know me a Texian, and your enemy!" He stands before the astonished company wearing the full garb of a Texan, with hunting shirt, bowie knife, and pistols at his belt.

The governor is stunned. "My eyes! Was ever such a stratagem!"

And Don Pedro shouts, "Upon the traitor!"

But Bonham brandishes his Colt revolver and confronts them with: "Upon him with what appetite you may! This little weapon counts a score of lives; each ready jaw is open for its victims." He turns first to one and then the other. "Who first? Is't you—or you—or you—? What, none!"

Before such a brash individual, so convincingly armed, the Mexicans fall back as Bonham's six-shooter singles out each one. The play ends happily with the Texans victorious and Bonham married to the beautiful Olivia.

The Texan plays before the Civil War were obviously the

great-grandsires of the movies treating Texans today. In the Hollywood version of the men of the Lone Star the Texans are cowboys who manage, before the final fadeout, to whip at least one tribe of Indians and an army of cattle rustlers as well, usually without reloading. A lady in distress is most often at hand to add a dash of romance. In the early plays the Texans were never cowboys, never had to chase rustlers off the ranch, and never gummed up the action by crooning a song. All those were details that came with the growth of the Texas cattle industry after the Civil War. But that is about as far as the difference goes. In personal characteristics, the Rangers and Alamo defenders on the nineteenth-century stage and the Texas cowpunchers on the twentieth-century screen are blood brothers.

Convention says that Texans before a theater audience must always champion the side of the right. That their strength and their Colts usually make them unbeatable in fighting for that right has long seemed to please everybody.

Vol. I. "*Go Ahead!*" **No. 3.**

Davy Crockett's
18 ALMANACK, 37
OF WILD SPORTS IN THE WEST,
Life in the Backwoods, & Sketches of Texas.

O KENTUCKY: THE HUNTERS OF KENTUCKY!!!

Nashville, Tennessee. Published by the heirs of Col. Crockett.

Almanacs were usually small in size, but cover designs
indicated mighty fabrications.

INFANT CROCKETT
EATING
HIS BREAKFAST

Crockett's Almanac
(New York, 1848)

". . . . as soon as I war weaned, I took to bear's meat in the most rantankerous manner, and made it fly without wings."

CROCKETT CATCHING
A MEXICAN TIGRESS

Crockett's Almanac
(Boston, 1846)

"Jist you foller me to the haunt of the crittur you want, an if I don't kidnap the hull tiger family, then call me a sucker fawn."

CHAPTER NINE

Warriors and the Weather

WHAT plays were to the cities, the comic almanacs were to the country at large. Outside of New York, Philadelphia, and the other large urban centers, few Americans ever saw Texan plays. But they early learned the ways of Texans through the almanacs which, for at least a half-century, kept America laughing.

These little books were popular because their contents were designed frankly to appeal to the greatest of American audiences, the uneducated mass mind. The average issue boasted a loose, often illogical, conglomeration of weather forecasts, household hints, farm lore, woodcuts, jokes, and funny stories. It was the humor in these "comic" almanacs that made them sell widely. The weather information and high and low tide figures, which were obviously relevant only to a restricted locality, would have sold comparatively few almanacs. But the jokes and the woodcuts greatly strengthened their bid for popularity, and many sold heavily in places far from the areas that could use the "facts" in them. Even in inland regions where their detailed tidal schedules were wholly beside the point, many of the comic almanacs were read and reread and laughed over heartily.

The Devil's Comical Texas Oldmanick (1836) was an almanac with such appeal. Its meteorological data were figured solely for the Philadelphia area, yet it carried a humorous treatment of Texas and Texans that guaranteed its sale far from the city of brotherly love. Knowing this, its editors took for the benefit of their public-at-large an amused attitude toward the weather forecast they included for June: "Depend upon weather; you'll not be disappointed; *heat expands all bodies;* therefore, as this is a warm month you may expect the days will be greatly lengthened, or more properly, greatly *expanded.*"[1]

As a picture of middle-class American life, the almanacs are unsurpassed; in details relating particularly to farm life they are especially rich. Several other types of printed material, such as magazines and newspapers, contain a wealth of information about the pre-Civil War American farmer; but the almanacs have a special value to social historians and to anyone else interested in tasting the life of the past, for these are, by and large, the only books that the farmers of a century ago were willing to pay good money for. A shelf of almanacs and a Bible comprised the library in most of America's rural homes. Each in its own way gave the kind of direction the public wanted, and if Scripture failed to lift the readers' loads completely, the jokes in the almanacs helped. The almanacs interested the whole family. The crudely drawn illustrations amused the children and grandparents unable to read, and the text entertained the rest.

As booklets that furnished many people their only reading matter, the comic almanacs were a great public's first and most memorable exposure to the bluster and boast of the Typical Texan. The almanacs that helped America to make up its mind about him were of two types. One played up the humor and high adventure in Texan life for their own sakes, without ulterior designs on the opinions of its readers. The other was the godchild of alert press agents and campaign managers who were quick to recognize the value of almanacs in spreading ideas. Though it would be hard today to prove that the almanacs were ever effective propaganda, there is no doubt that politicians put them to use.

The campaign almanac that featured Texans most colorfully was the *Rough and Ready Almanac*, designed to make Zachary Taylor President. Issues of this almanac were published in each of the two years preceding the election of 1848. By emphasizing the battles of the Mexican War in which Taylor had fought, his campaign managers sought to imply that the North Mexican clashes were the most strategic victories of the war. The stories they included in the *Rough and Ready Almanac* were mostly reprinted eyewitness accounts which had been published earlier in book form and in such popular journals as the *New York Spirit of the Times*. The same was true of the illustrations. Perhaps these almanacs helped to carry Taylor to the White House. Perhaps they did not, though the chances seem good that these little books, which played up the fighting qualities that had already endeared Taylor to many close observers of his part in the Mexican War, did their share toward his victory. Like the *Rough and Ready Melodists,* little campaign songbooks which resembled them, the almanacs helped plant nationally the nickname, "Old Rough and Ready," which turned out to be excellent politics. The editors also showed themselves to be good students of public taste when they described Taylor in Mexico against a background of Texas Rangers.

Both issues of the *Rough and Ready* are filled with spirited descriptions of the Rangers fighting in Monterrey and along the Rio Grande. The Rangers posed great discipline problems for the officers in Taylor's command, and though the General recognized their service in defeating the enemy in northern Mexico, he was tremendously relieved when most of the unruly Texans were mustered out of his disciplined ranks. But the campaign managers glossed over that smudge on the Texans' record and glamorized them fully in the election literature they passed around. In the *Rough and Ready* almanacs, at least, the Texans could do no wrong. The Rangers with their leaders—Jack Hays, Ben McCulloch, Samuel Walker—are pictured, both in the drawings and in the text, as supermen.

The second *Rough and Ready* issue was devoted almost entirely to the Texas Rangers. Based principally on Reid's *Scouting Expeditions of McCulloch's Texas Rangers,* its articles spotlighted the activities of Walker, Hays, and McCulloch. McCulloch figures here in a biographical sketch and a drawing. A former Tennesseean, McCulloch had intended to go to Texas with Crockett but was too late to join his party at Nacogdoches, and thus missed death at the Alamo and was alive to distinguish himself as the leader of a Ranger company in the Mexican War. Jack Hays was featured in two articles, one a biography, the other a three-page report on his fights with Indians. An

Indian chief quoted in the report paid tribute to Captain Jack Hays's bravery by saying: "Blue Wing and I no fraid to go to *hell* together—'Captain Jack,' great brave—no fraid to go to *hell* by himself."[2]

Though not mentioned by name, other Rangers are clearly described in these pages as courageous champions of liberty. One of Walker's Rangers, recently returned home from the war, was describing the battles he had fought in when a lad among the listeners slapped his thigh and shouted: "Damn me if I don't go to the wars!"

Attracted by this outburst, the Texan turned. Seeing that the speaker was a small, delicate-looking boy, he said to him: "*You* go to the wars!—hum, you had better stay home!"

"Yes, *me*,—why not *me?*" the lad cried, drawing himself up to his full height.

"Why, thar is a heap to do out thar, youngster," said the Ranger, "which you mought not be able to do, that's all."

"And what have *you* done?" queried the boy, looking up at the Texan, who stood over six feet tall.

The crowd gathered around, anxiously leaning forward to catch the Texan's reply.

"What have *I* done?" The Texan repeated the question several times, laying much stress on the *I*. "What have *I* done, why," said he, "I have done more than you will ever do, if *you* go."

"And what is *that?*" asked the boy.

"Why, I've got back safe!" said the Texan, with a loud laugh of triumph in which the crowd joined.[3]

The readers of the *Rough and Ready* almanacs had reason to think that "getting back safe" was characteristic of all Texas Rangers.

Not all the comic almanacs painted so favorable a picture of Texans. "G.T.T." was too convenient to the purposes of the joke-makers to be ignored. *The Devil's Comical Texas Oldmanick: with Comic Engravings of all the Principal Events of Texas* played this theme for all that it was worth. Most of its pages demonstrated how thoroughly the Texans outshone the Mexicans, but the general hint throughout this almanac is that the Texas army was composed mostly of rogues and refugees from the United States. The illustration, "Houston's Address to His Army," could hardly have expressed the gibe more eloquently. It pictures a listless Houston delivering to a ragged, ill-assorted group of derelicts this wondrously mild speech:

"Soldiers, there is the enemy. Do you want to fight?"

"Yes."

"Well, then, let us eat our dinners, and then I will lead you into the battle."[4]

Fisher's Comic Almanac for 1841 carried a Wall Street conversation that embodied another aspect of the same anti-Texas attitude:

"How are you, B.? What's the news? Do you know how stocks sold today?"

"I only know that I bought none. Have you got five hundred dollars you could let me have till next Wednesday?"

"No, have you?"

"No. Why doesn't the Great Western [a transatlantic ship] come along?"

"I wonder if the Bank of England has suspended specie payment."

"Nonsense. How is cotton?"

"Bad. We are a ruined nation. I have a mind to put G. T. T. on my cards and clear out for Texas."[5]

The Old American Comic Almanac for 1843 echoed Fisher. A husband reporting his domestic troubles to a judge said his wife's main fault was her addiction to the bottle. The judge said: "Lock it away from her."

"She's got all the keys."

"Don't let her have any money."

"She keeps all the cash."

"Well then," said the judge, "part from her."

"She won't let me."

"Then I don't know what to advise. There's only one course—run off to Texas, for that is the land of promise for every rogue, fool, and discontented person here."[6]

The almanac failed to report what decision the husband came to, but it is doubtful whether a person of his passive nature could have been much happier in Texas where, according to

Davy Crockett, every man had to "stand up to his lick log" or die.

The series of almanacs which featured Davy Crockett's escapades were among the most active spreaders of the Texan Tradition. Some historians have been eager to read great political significance into them, and not without some reason. First issued by a Nashville publisher in 1834,[7] the "Crocketts" were consistently pro-West throughout the twenty-odd years of their popularity. Much of their humor was based on the average westerner's scorn, or pity, for anybody else. Hence the Crocketts, with an obviously sectional approach, were indirectly political. And the 1846 and 1849 numbers did actively support the expansionists' dreams of an America stretching to 54-40. But that is about as propagandist as the Crockett series ever became. Most of the numbers simply exhibit a section ready to laugh at its neighbors and willing enough to laugh at itself.

More than the newspaper stories and the books Crockett wrote or was said to have written, the almanacs bearing his name fostered the legends that formed about the Coonskin Congressman and hero of the Alamo. Next to nothing is known of the men who produced them. There is no proof that David Crockett actually was ever active in their production, though a writer in the 1837 issue says that its sketches about Texas came from letters which Crockett wrote home, and Crockett was said to have prepared in advance before he left Tennessee enough material to fill six full issues. The truth of this has not been determined, and some students have always doubted it. Harvard's Howard Mumford Jones says that those, whoever they were, who originated the Crockett almanac stories were skilful literary technicians, for they often reproduced faithfully the peculiar speech of the backwoods,[8] and many of their speech figures often approach the magnificent. As literature, much of the writing in the Crocketts is poetic, full of the turbulence, the earthy energy, and the recklessness of the unlettered people who read them.

The years between 1834 and 1856, the date of the last known issue, saw Crockett almanacs bearing the imprints of publishers in Nashville, Baltimore, Boston, Philadelphia, and New York. In all some fifty issues appeared.[9] This was an unusually healthy career for a comic almanac. Its popularity for such a long period proves that the humor, the woodcuts, the fantastic yarns delighted thousands in whose imaginations Davy Crockett could not die. And it is indirect evidence, at least, that the almanac public liked what it found in the Crocketts about Texas.

Many passages in the Crockett almanacs contributed directly to the stature of the Typical Texan. So also did their illustrations. Their specific comments about the Texans, and the Texan characters who appeared in them, were very little more important in the tradition's emergence than were the suggestions of the Texan world and life contained in the drawings and the "feel" of many of the articles. The Crockett almanacs and their stirring drawings probably cemented the relationship between Crockett and the Typical Texan more firmly than any of the other media which caused them to be associated in the American popular mind. Certainly these almanacs were the most widely read treatment of Crockett among Texans on their own ground.

Unlike the Yankees, the Indians, the Negroes, and other "foreigners," Texans received friendly treatment in the Crocketts. The over-all picture of Texas and the Texans falls roughly into two divisions. The first shows Texas to be a fabulous country equal to the tall tales about it. The second describes the Texan as a superb fighting man.

Taking a cue from Mrs. Holley, Crockett in his Nashville issue for 1837 praises Texas' fertility as vigorously as do most devoted Texans today: "Talking of crops, they say Texas is the place; and the land is so rich, if you plant a crowbar at night it will sprout tenpenny nails before morning." Compared to Texas, "our land in West Tennessee is merely frog pasture."[10] Such talk was a magnificent compliment to Texas, as any regular reader of Davy's almanac well knew, for if Davy Crockett was willing to rank Texas above Tennessee, no one could doubt that he had found it an "all-beatin'" place. It was the "green corner of Mrs. Liberty's garden," a place "whar all the wild game flies right to

you," and "whar a single ear of corn will make an injun puddin
big enough to feed a hull family, swine an all."[11]

The reputation of the Typical Texan himself is linked with
the almanac treatment of Texas' fertile soil and her extraordinary animals. In Texas, where such things abounded, ordinary
people would have seemed like lambs a long way from the fold.
The almanacs proclaimed that the Texan was a match, in all
respects, for the natural wonders of his land.

According to the Crocketts, Texas was home to a whole menagerie of amazing creatures. The drawings of these monsters
prove them to have been remarkable enough, but Crockett's
verbal descriptions rank them with nine-headed hydras and
minotaurs.

Of all the feathered critters that Crockett ever saw, the
"Texian Condor" was the most "tearifferous and tigeracious."
Really, he was like no bird—or anything else—Davy had thus far
stumbled on. The beast was so "all furious savage in his disposi-
tion" that it seemed he must have in him a mixture of "wolf vul-
ture," "brute buzzard," and panther. He could snap a thunderbolt out of joint. His claws were equal to two harrows jammed
together, and his bill was like a "patent double high pressure
blacksmith's vice." The way he liked to torture and tantalize human flesh was enough to put your teeth on edge; in fact, it
turned Crockett's into knife blades just to think about it.[12]

The panther that stole geese from Davy's pen "up near the
great fork o' Red River" made Crockett so angry that his skin
"crawled." When the "cretur" looked him in the face as innocent as if he had never filched a goose in all his life, Crockett's
hair stood up "like pine groves in winter." Davy thought it was
too merciful to shoot him, so he just put a rope over his legs,
tied him up, and then shaved all the hair off his body "from
his nose to the end o' his pesky tail." He kept up such a "terrifi-
cacious" yelling all the time that they heard it clear up in Pine
Hollow. When Crockett finally turned him loose, with all his
hair shaved off, the panther's skin "war smooth as a gal's cheek,
and the crittur didn't know what to do. He kept turning round
and round, and was so ashamed that he kivered up his face with

his paws." Crockett's wife and daughters laughed uproariously when they saw him, and the panther ran off into the forest— and, Crockett said, "I don't think he ever cum back into them parts, for the crittur war ashamed to be seen."[13]

Only a hero like Crockett could have conquered the rattle-snakes he met in Texas. His almanac for 1846 carries the account of his battle with them: "You've no doubt all heard what an all exterminator Saint Patrick was among snakes and toads, but if he'd been in America, he wouldn't have found out his great snake exilein business quite so easy, unless he did it altogether on the Crockett plan." On a beautiful thousand-acre tract in Texas, the six- and eight-foot rattlers were so thick that "no arthly crittur but birds could venter within a hundred yards o' the spot without being cut up into rattle snake chews like to-bacco." Crockett continues, "Why, take my body for ship-timber if the tarnal drummen sarpents didn't use up more injuns than whiskey, or the square toed small pox, and they kept the buzz-ards so tarnal fat on beast meat that they couldn't fly." So, not liking to see so much useless destruction, and thinking it a shame that such good land was going to waste, Crockett thought he would just take a walk in among the serpents and show them that all the snake-killers were not in Ireland. With some Indians to guide him to the spot, Crockett made ready to "walk into 'em like fire among prairie grass." Since he always gave every crea-ture, even a snake, a fair chance, Crockett shook his "teeth to-gether by way of a warning rattle, an they answered with a shake that would have made you think that the airth, trees, and all war rattle snakes." He then waded into them, grabbing a half-dozen in each hand. He cracked them up and down "suddenaci-ously whip fashion" until their heads flew off through the air as thick as snowflakes, "till the hull nation war exterminated, and the injuns run up cheerin, 'Saint Davy Crockett,' amidst such a shower o' snakes heads as were never seen afore."[14]

Crockett's Devil Buffalo, the most hair-raising animal in the almanac for 1854, was fit company for rattlers and Texian con-dors. He was a "savagerous and feroficacious" beast measuring twenty feet long and ten feet high. He kept up a continual thunderstorm half the year round and could scare away the sunrise when he wanted to. Consequently, men called him "the Buffalo Devil, that no critter could go for to kum at." Shouldering his gun one morning, Crockett went out in search of the monster, and, Davy says, "he proved to be a devil for sarten— for when he first put his fire-eye on me, he looked like Mount Aetna in a state of eruption. I fust let my dogs fly at him, but they war no use, for the crittur gave one snort o' red-fire, and they war singed up for life." So Crockett walked right up to him, pulled out his tail, and beat him with it until he dropped down in convulsions.[15]

The "bedeviled bison," by the way, appeared twenty-four years later in a narrative featuring Strap Buckner in Taylor and McDanield's travel account, *The Coming Empire: or 2000 Miles in Texas on Horseback* (1878). Crockett's superbuffalo is similar to the bull disguise the Devil assumed to whip Strap Buckner, the mighty Texan folk hero. There is probably no way to establish the debt these travelers owed to the almanac, but the resemblance of their story to the Crockett tale is close enough to make one think they had read it and revised it to their own ends.

According to the almanac issues which chronicle Crockett's career in Texas, his adventures there began long before he met the Mexican army at the Alamo. One day he rode out to look at the country to "see if thar war any varmints astir thar." Passing a tract of timber, he saw two Mexicans galloping toward him, apparently intending to run him down. Giving his reins a jerk, he moved his horse a little to one side, and as the Mexicans were both going by, rammed his bowie knife into the side of one of them. The Mexican wheeled his horse to return, but Davy drew a bead on his left eye and fired, and the Mexican fell into the mud. It was all over so quickly that Crockett thought it must have been a dream.

At another time when his friend Jimmie Raymond, "the wild beast collector for all creation," wanted fifty men to accompany him into Mexico to catch a female tiger, Crockett fell into such a fit of laughter that it nearly shook the clothes off his back.

"Jist you foller me to the haunt of the crittur you want," he said, "an if I don't kidnap the hull tiger family, then call me a sucker fawn." Raymond agreed, and off they started. When they came near a dark swamp, Crockett saw "a couple o' small lights which turned out to be a he tiger's eyes keeping watch for his wife an family." The tiger was just in the act of springing when Crockett caught hold of his front paws, twisted them, and "tied 'em around his neck so tarnal tight, that he died an choked instanter." Crockett then proceeded into the lair, grabbed "Mrs. Tiger" by the throat, pared off her nails, and held her until he had choked half her temper out; then he put her young ones in his skin cap and marched out, "draggen their mammy arter me by the throat as docile as a kitten."[16]

This was only a warm-up for Crockett's battle with a lion in a Mexican arena, where as a prisoner he was forced to fight. He conquered the lion by clinching his "thumb nails right through his juggler, . . . and arter one sewaggerous hug, and Kentucky clinch," he hurled the panting varmint to the ground.[17]

At length the characteristics of Davy and the Typical Texan became so nearly identical that in at least one instance a story first told about a Texan came to be regarded as a Crockett tale. *Crockett's Almanac* for 1848 (Boston) carries an account of Davy's roasting a buffalo steak on a prairie fire. The story closely resembles the contents of a letter written at least two years before by George W. Kendall to the *New Orleans Picayune*. In Kendall's version the story was about a soldier in the Mexican War, "Bill Dean, the Texan Ranger." His letter may well have been the source of this "Crockett" tale. If it was, this is an example of a Texan narrative contributing to the Crockett legend, and perhaps it sheds some light on the methods of the almanac-makers.

When one of his horses died, we read, Dean and his men decided to eat it. The horse was easily butchered, but cooking it presented a problem. Dean "piled up a heap of prairie grass, for it was high and dry, and set it on fire; but it flashed up like powder, and went out as quick." But the fire caught the high grass close by, and the wind carried the flames streaking across the prairie. Dean reported: "I followed up the fire, holding my chunk of meat directly over the blaze, . . . I chased that d——d fire a mile and a half, . . . and never give it up until I run plumb into a wet marsh; there the fire and the chunk of horsemeat came out even—a dead heat, especially the meat."[18]

In the almanac version, Crockett heard a buffalo coming toward him as if a "harrycane war blowing him along." He shot it and cut off a rump steak, expecting to eat it raw, when he saw a fire sweeping across the prairie. As it roared past him, he stuck the steak on the end of his bowie knife and ran along holding the steak up to the fire. "I kep up with it," says Crockett, "till the steak war roasted as well as I ever seed it done at any hotel in Washington when I war in Congress. I sot down on the ground, and Growler [his dog] sot up on eend by the side of me, and the way that we poked the fat steak into our eating-holes, war prodigious."[19]

Crockett's adventures prior to his arrival in San Antonio were simple tussles compared to his fighting activities as a defender of the Alamo. In this role Crockett made his greatest contribution to the reputation of the Texans, for the almanacs, like the plays, treat Crockett at the Alamo as a full-fledged Texan, battling not for personal glory, but wholeheartedly for the Texan cause.

Crockett's fighting apprenticeship among the canebrakes and gum forests of Tennessee was a valuable preparation for the bloody encounter he faced at the Alamo. His old trick of grinning and screaming an opponent down failed him against the Mexicans, but his trusty rifle "Kill-Devil" (or "Betsey"), his bowie knife "Big Butcher," his vicelike grip, and his thumbnails served him well at various times during the struggle.

While his ammunition lasted, Crockett, singlehanded, fought like a full platoon. When his gun became red hot from steady firing, he quit bothering to pull the trigger or to take aim, for the gun went off automatically and bagged a Mexican every time. *The Devil's Comical Texas Oldmanick* said that during the siege Crockett killed 85 men and wounded 120. "As he was one of the best Rifle Shooters of the West, and had four rifles, with two men to load constantly, . . . he brought down his man as fast as they could load."[20]

At close quarters with the Mexicans, the greatly outnumbered Texans depended upon their fists, knives, and sharp-toed boots as much as their muskets. Crockett admitted that "it war a tuff time in Tecksass then, but we stood up to our lick log till we licked the pesky Spanyards as clean as a barked hemlock." "Kill-Devil" spoke out like an earthquake "roarin' on a wager." When his ammunition was gone, Crockett swung away with the breech of his musket, and when the gun splintered, he fell to with his thumbnail. Crockett said,

> I war horrid mad and swore most butiful. One drummer tride to stop me; I kicked his drum a rod, and cotch his face in both my hands, and twisted it up like a cork screw so that he never could see himself arterward without lookin' in a crooked looking glass, and if he war to foller his nose, he would be obliged to run around in a circle. I went thro' 'em like a steembote with seven bilers, I spit so hard at one feller that I broke his jaw with a chaw of tobakker.[21]

For all Crockett's ingenuity, death finally claimed him at the Alamo in 1836. The 1837 almanac (Nashville) says his body was found in an angle of two buildings with his dagger in his hand, surrounded by seventeen dead Mexicans. In the dark he had had a definite advantage over them, since they could not get behind him, and he stabbed them as they passed. But he finally was reached by two musket balls, and as he fell, a smile of scorn played on his lips. Another version of his death, in the 1848 almanac (Boston), has him stabbed first by one of the wounded men at his feet, and then run through with a bayonet from behind, "for the crittur would as soon have faced a hundred live mammoths as to have faced Crockett at any time."[22]

Many of the almanacs swore that he never died. In *Ben Hardin's Crockett Almanac* for 1842 (Baltimore) the mighty backwoodsman, alive and without a scratch, turns up at the Battle of San Jacinto. His repeated resurrection in the almanac stories and others current about him prompted a dialogue in *Bone Squash's Black Joke Al-Ma-Nig for de Year Arter Last* (1852): "Sambo, why am Daby Crockett like a cat?" "Why,

Cuff, kase he got nine libes." At San Jacinto, Crockett had a "hellniferous time; and I thort I war a gone sucker, for the pettiferous Spanyards drawed up around me, and six on 'em drew a lead on me at wunst." The rest began to play possum, Crockett says, "and I should ha' got cleer of 'em very soon, but thar cum up a fresh gang; and I shot one of 'em, but they crowded in upon me, and razed me off my feet. So when I fell down, they jumpt on me, but before they could ty my hands, I had my thum-nale into the eye of 'em."[23]

This time Crockett was captured and taken in chains to a salt mine in Mexico where his captors had the "imperdence to expect me to work with a harty good will for 'em." But the almanacs, with the freedom of folklore, deliver him from his bonds to shout for America's westward expansion, the annexation of Texas, and the Mexican War.

In 1845 Crockett's indignation ran high against Mexico:

Considering Texas as one o' the stars that belonged to Uncle Sam's Striped Handkerchief, I swore, by the hem in Freedom's buckskin petticoat, that Santa Anna or any other tyrant should never wipe his nose with it; . . . I recollected the all-bloody lickin' I gin him at Alamo, buckled on my old scythe which he knows is about equal to old death, and prepared to start off instanterly to carve the whiskered critter right up.[24]

In 1847 he calls for all patriotic Americans to join in the fight to stop Mexico's abuse of Texas. He lists many grievances against the enemy and says America should "pierce the heart of the enemy as you would a feller that spit in your face, knocked down your wife, burnt up your houses, and called your dog a skunk."[25]

To the Texans and to America at large Crockett shouts:

Hosses, I am with you! And while the stars of Uncle Sam, and the stripes of his country triumphantly wave in the breeze,—whar,—whar,—whar is the craven, low-lived, chicken-bred, toad-hoppin, red-mounted, bristle-headed mother's son of ye who will not raise the beacon light of triumph,—smouse the citadel of the aggressor, and squeeze ahead for Liberty and Glory! Whoop! h -w -rah, hosses, come along,—Crockett's with you,—show us the inemy![26]

The Rangers in the Mexican War could not have asked for a better cohort than this Crockett of the almanacs. And nobody's imagination needs to stretch far to see the fiendish delight on old Davy's face if he could have been on hand to walk through the walls of Monterrey with them. They were all fighters, cut from the same rough homespun, all charged with the same dauntless spirits. They would have been proud to ride in the same company.

In the minds of men today, they do.

CHAPTER TEN

Riding the Bookmen's Bandwagon

THOUGH he has always had as little truck with book learning as possible, since about 1840 the Typical Texan has seldom been missing from the world of books. Then as now, readers could find him without much trouble in a volume at a price they were willing to pay—two or three dollars for a novel bound in boards, a quarter or less for one in paper. For your money you seldom got much quality. But if you bought these books you were after dash, and that they supplied in plenty.

Romantic souls like Mrs. Viele hailed Texas as the likeliest new source of romance in American letters. She was convinced that "to a mind like Cooper's, Texas opens a new field, full of intense and varied interest for the novel writer."[1] Many writers of "intense and varied" interests put Texas to use in their own special ways. None came up with any fiction equal to Cooper's best, but a sizable public in the 1840's and 1850's did not care. If these writers lacked Cooper's gifts for character portrayal, they approached him in ability to whip up exciting plots out of Indians and frontiersmen in the wilderness.

Texans arrived on the fiction scene at a time of fundamental change in book publishing. Texan stories have been in print almost as long as there has been an independent American publishing trade. Before the introduction of Sir Walter Scott's novels in this country in the 1820's, the novel as a craft practiced by Americans had hardly learned how to stand alone. Certainly it was far from taking its first steps as a genuine concern of American publishers. The fiction that achieved the widest popularity in America was primarily the offering of English publishers who looked to the United States as their principal foreign market. Booksellers here welcomed the English imprints, since the mechanical means for producing books on this side of the Atlantic were years behind methods used in England, and there-

CROCKETT ROASTING A BUFFALO STEAK BY THE PRAIRIE FIRE

Crockett's Almanac (New York, 1848)

"I kep up with it till the steak war roasted as well as I ever seed it at any
hotel in Washington when I war in Congress."

CROCKETT KILLING RATTLESNAKES

*Crockett's Almanac
(Boston, 1846)*

"I then went into 'em like
flax pullin, . . . an holden
'em up, jirked down sud-
denaciously whip fashion
and cracked 'em till thar
heads flew off through the
air as thick as snow-flakes."

Price 25 Cents.

THE
PRAIRIE GUIDE,

BY NEWTON M. CURTIS, ESQ.

NEW-YORK:
W. F. BURGESS, No. 22 ANN-STREET.

CINCINNATI, OHIO.
BURGESS & WOOD, No. 149 MAIN-STREET.

Novelettes were similar in style and size to the Almanacs
but added chivalry to the almanac idea of Texans.

fore the price of American books was often all but prohibitive.

Until transportation and communication began to catch up with modern times in the 1820's, American publishing was the business of the small shop. Selling at any distance was difficult. Thus the average publisher restricted his efforts to a comparatively small area. Here he met little competition, and his relations with others of his craft were, on the whole, amicable.[2]

But this was before Scott. About the time Scott's Waverley novels began to excite American readers, transportation facilities in this country had improved enough to make it possible for booksellers to market their wares in regions which until then had been beyond reach. At the same time mechanical innovations began to have a profound effect on the domestic manufacture of books. Steam power could now be utilized to drive the presses, printers learned stereotyping techniques that allowed them to use a single set of type in printing great numbers of books, paper was easier to make and cheaper. The processes of binding were also improved. For the book trade the future was bright; the happy day of large printings of low-priced editions was now at hand.

Since there was as yet no such thing as an international copyright law, nothing could prevent the country's being flooded with pirated editions of popular English works. Publishing was no longer a dignified business based on ethical rules. The successful publishers now were often those shrewdest in cutting competitors' throats. The publisher's profits depended largely on his skill in getting to the source of supply, the English booksellers, ahead of his rivals. Mathew Carey's publishing firm in Philadelphia boasted in 1823 that twenty-eight hours after it received a copy of Scott's latest novel, *Quentin Durward,* it had 1,500 reprints ready for sale. Carey knew that forty-eight hours after his edition was on the streets his competitors would be ready with their own reprints taken from his; but he felt that the few days' advantage in the bookshops would justify the frenzy attached to publishing a book in such haste.[3]

This is where Texans came in. In the struggle for domination in the piracy field Park Benjamin in 1839 and Jonas Winchester in 1840 adopted a highly original scheme. They edited respectively the weeklies *Brother Jonathan* and the *New World*. These huge sheets, which sold for a few cents, were four-page affairs measuring four feet in length and eleven columns in width. They specialized in pirated serial editions of such popular foreign authors as Dickens, Bulwer, and Captain Marryat, and in the works of fly-by-night American authors. Since the instalment weeklies soon proved too slow to compete with the speedy new methods of bookmakers, Benjamin and Winchester began retaliating by issuing small "extras," numbering seventy or eighty closely printed pages, which carried their novels complete. These booklets sold for as little as five or six cents a copy. Other mammoths like the *Flag of Our Union* and the *Weekly Yankee* soon sprang up to compete with them.

Few Americans dared to risk publishing an American novel of quality that would have to sell for two dollars against the competition of a pirated British novel selling for a dollar and a half, or against one of the five-cent extras. The American author was protected from his fellow American writers by a domestic copyright, but this gave him no protection whatever from foreign competition. Only Washington Irving and the "American Scott," James Fenimore Cooper, could hold their own commercially against the cheap reprints and the hack work of American writers. Consequently, as late as 1829 no "literary" author was supporting himself by his pen in New York.[4] And this indicated the state of serious writers throughout the country.

To compete with the cheap publications, many talented American writers turned frankly hack. The field of domestic fiction which grew out of the extras of big weeklies specializing in melodramatic adventure stories offered them money, if not artistic satisfaction. Like many others, Joseph Holt Ingraham, who became one of the most economically successful American writers, courted popularity and financial reward at the expense of critical respect by writing "novelettes," some of which, at twenty-five cents apiece, sold forty or fifty thousand copies

and more. Ingraham was, by the way, one of the earliest writers
to delve in the unworked veins of romance in Texas and the
Southwest. E. Z. C. Judson ("Ned Buntline"), another writer
of Texan novelettes, swallowed whatever pride he may have had
and recognized the compromise required of a professional literary man. "I found that to *make a living,*" Judson wrote, "I
must write 'trash' for the masses, for he who endeavors to write
for the critical few, and do his genius justice, will go hungry if
he has no other means of support."[5] Judson became so adept at
turning out his "trash" that during one six-day stretch he
spouted ten thousand words a day.[6] Over a long period he
earned $20,000 a year.[7] Another writer of Texan novelettes,
Henry William Herbert, who wrote *Pierre, the Partisan,* was
one of the first writers in America to support himself solely by
his pen,[8] by writing, according to Edgar Allan Poe, "more trash
than any man living, with the exception of [Theodore S.] Fay."[9]

The Texan paperbacks, or novelettes, which these men and
their associates "manufactured" were a direct result of the un-
abashed commercialism which characterized the publishing
world at the time when Texas began to claim widespread
interest.

When Charles Wilkins Webber was a boy in Kentucky, he
and his playmates delighted in listening to the tales the stage
passengers told while fresh horses were being harnessed. If the
traveler was on his way from Texas or Mexico, Webber says,
"we watched him with awe and wonder."[10] It was just such boys
as these, along with their older brothers and their parents as
well, who bought the paperbacks forty or fifty thousand strong.

These stories were never intended to be accurate portrayals
of life in Texas. The novelette writers were interested only in
packing their plots with as much exciting adventure as possible. The sober domestic details of life on the home front would
have bored their readers, and the authors left them strictly
alone. Women over their washtubs, farmers at their plows, children, and the hundred other aspects of mundane life in Texas
were nonexistent as far as these writers were concerned. In their
books the only Texans alive were he-men on horseback, never

for long tied down by either apron strings, responsibilities, or the finer points of the law. They were the breed of men that Stephen Crane some decades later used in his story, "A Man and—Some Others." When Bill, a Texan, reports that some Mexicans are planning to drive him off the range, his listener, a newcomer, says, "Well, why in the name of wonder don't you go get the sheriff?"

"Oh, hell!" says Bill, in supreme disgust.

The novelettes all looked about alike. Bound in yellow paper, the average one numbered a hundred pages of eye-punishing print in double columns. The paper was rough and became brittle quickly. Though their original editions sometimes reached sixty thousand, these books are rare today because of the poor quality of the paper on which they were printed. Durability interested neither the publishers nor the customers. The volumes served their purpose if they held together long enough so that a few people could read them. They were not meant for immortality in a library, and they seldom received such reward.

The earliest of the Texan paperbacks was James Wilmer Dallam's *The Lone Star; a Tale of Texas; Founded upon Incidents in the History of Texas,* published in New York in 1845. Dallam's name is more often connected with legislative affairs in Texas during its republic and early statehood periods than with fiction. Born in Baltimore in 1818, he could well write from experience about the problems of migrating to Texas and settling there. His death at twenty-nine from yellow fever ended a career of some promise in this type of literature. *The Lone Star* is a tempestuous tale of heroics and villainy along the coastal plain between Houston and the Rio Grande. Dallam says in his preface that the main incidents in the plot are true and that many of them were records of his own personal experience. He declares further that they can bear no imputation of fiction, beyond that which the "laws of pure romance" readily justify.

After such a prologue, the reader would be foolish to expect a convincing tale of reality. The book is, nevertheless, a fair picture of the mixed collection of newcomers to Texas and the motives that prompted their coming. The action takes place just after the Alamo defeat when Texas, claiming independence from Mexico, was continually nettled by bands of Mexican guerrillas. Walter Deane, an adventurer, and his son Roland journey to Texas to aid her in her fight. Every newspaper they had read had teemed with incitements to aid the Texans; so, motivated by an "ardent and honest love of liberty," they set out for Texas, to answer a "call of duty which it would be wrong to disobey."[11] In Roland, Dallam personified once and for all the typical hero of Texan fiction. "He was tall and thin, yet well proportioned; and, despite the shabby and rather uncouth figure he presented in his buck-skin pantaloons and short round jacket, was evidently handsome. His keen, dark blue eye flashed momentarily with an expression of vigilance and uneasiness."[12] His effects included a horn drinking cup, a powder flask, a silver-handled bowie knife, and a pair of silver-mounted pistols.

A series of successful fights with the Mexicans composes the plot, which concerns itself with the brave efforts of the Texans to conquer the wilderness and to wrest their country from Mexican tyranny. Convinced that his future lies in Texas, Roland marries and decides to remain there.

Dallam was well aware of the popularity of Scott's novels and the world of chivalry they pictured. In his *Lone Star* he points out the resemblance of Texan adventures to those of medieval knighthood. "Neither tilt nor tournament, nor tented field can furnish ingredients, more glowing, more animating, or more instructing, than the waving plumes of the Indians, dancing in ten thousand mazes above the verdant prairie." One would have to search far and wide, says Dallam, to find a more exciting picture than "the varying courses of the almost eternal horsemen, when curvetting, in their wild majesty and grandeur, preparatory to their bold and resistless sweep, across the battle field."[13]

The Texan Rangers came in for their earliest fictional treatment in Joseph Holt Ingraham's *The Texan Ranger; or, the Maid of Matamoras, a Tale of the Mexican War* (1846). The book was typical of Ingraham's work during the period when he was writing steadily for the cheap publications. Though the editor of the *Knickerbocker* dismissed the "literary pretensions of

'Professor' Ingraham" as lamentable evidence of the furniture of the author's mind,[14] such "pretensions" troubled only the serious critics. Edgar Allan Poe recognized Ingraham as one of America's most popular novelists, "if not one of our best."[15] Announcing a new Ingraham story soon to be published serially in the *New York Morning Star*, the *Weekly Yankee* reported that that paper would accordingly start printing ten thousand extra copies. Serialized in the newspapers, Ingraham's novels paid him more than three thousand dollars a year.[16] In 1846 he told the poet Longfellow that he had written eighty novels, twenty during the past year, and that writing had become merely mechanical with him. *The Texan Ranger*, one of the twenty, was surely written as mechanically as any. Nevertheless, the Rangers show up well in it.

Ingraham describes them as remarkable gunfighters. When the Ranger captain sees the Mexican "hussars" advancing, he shouts to his men: "My boys, you see what they are. There is no end to them as they advance into sight over the ridge! there are not less than three hundred Mexicans; we are seventy Texans." He reminds them that San Jacinto proved "one Texan to be equal to seven Mexicans; and we fairly out-number these fellows by my arithmetic."[17] In the battle that follows, two Rangers chase twenty of the hussars a mile, and five others put thirty to rout. After they have chased off the full three hundred, the Ranger captain laughs and says, "Now, my boys, never after this say one and one make two, but five and one make two; one Texan and five Mexicanos. This is Rangers' arithmetic."

Lucy Morley: or, the Young Officer; a Tale of the Texan Revolution (1846), by "Miss Alice Cleveland," is the story of George Newcomb, a young New Yorker, "too true a patriot" to heed his father's opposition, who leads a company of volunteers to help the Texans. The plot conforms to a pattern common in these stories: the hero leaves a dull routine in the United States to fight the enemies of Texas. Eventually he must decide whether to return home or to remain where the prospects are bright, in Texas. Newcomb decides to take his timorous bride to New York where she can forget the nightmares of life in the

Texan forests. But many of the men who went to Texas with him stay on.

The story is full of fighting, but the main emphasis is placed on the courtesy of the Texan adventurers toward women. Throughout the action, which revolves around their efforts to put down the Kiowas and Mexicans who have been terrorizing the women, Newcomb and his friends all behave like perfect gentlemen. In becoming skilled fighters, they have lost none of their innate charm with the ladies. All the women in this story are the trembling maidens characteristic of the period's border romances. The Texans protect them gallantly.

Though it became famous as a play, Charles Wilkins Webber's *Jack Long: or, Shot in the Eye; a True Story of Texas Border Life* (1846) was more popular as a novelette. At nineteen, Webber had left home to wander along the wild frontiers of Texas. He knew Jack Hays and the Texas Rangers and had accompanied them in raids which he later described in his *Tales of the Southern Border* (1853). In 1844 he went to New York, determined to become a writer. Through John James Audubon and William Cullen Bryant he met Jonas Winchester, editor of the *New World*, who hired him to write a series of sketches on his Texas experiences. Later he wrote for the *Literary World*, the *Democratic Review*, the *Sunday Dispatch*, and *Graham's*. He maintained an abiding interest in the West, an interest strangely composed of romance and half-baked economics. A case in point is his connection with a gold expedition to the Gila River country; when the project failed because horses could not stand up to the long journey over deserts and mountain passes, Webber hit on the plan of using camels as beasts of burden in the Southwest.[18]

Like other American authors of his day, Webber suffered from the lack of international copyright law.[19] In the version of "Jack Long" in his *Tales of the Southern Border* he complains that "the millions of copies of this story which have been circulated in this country through the daily and weekly press" were taken from a mutilated pirated British edition.[20]

In Webber's story Jack Long, the Texan, had already pushed

ahead of two states and a territory and was typical of the "wild turkey breed," westerners who never stayed long in one place. Jack always settled wherever he chose, no matter who owned the land. "His heritage had been the young earth, with its skies, its waters, and its winds, its huge primeval forests, and plains throwing out their broad breasts to the sun . . . what cared he for the authority of men!"[21] The story describes Long's reactions when human authority unjustly punishes him. According to Webber, Sam Houston, when asked to send a civil force to stop the Regulators War in Shelby County, replied, "Fight it out among yourselves, and be d——d to you!"—a reaction, he says, "entirely characteristic of the man and the country as it then was!"[22] Webber gives Long credit for restoring law and order singlehanded, once he has shot the last of the Regulators through the eye.

As literature, the story is little better than the usual paperback tale, although it is true that Webber created in Long a character interesting in his own right and not simply a puppet in a melodrama. Both as a play and as a novelette, *Jack Long* was undoubtedly a strong influence in establishing the idea that Texans invariably stuck up for their rights. In looks and manner, Long fitted exactly the conception easterners had formed about backwoodsmen from observing such westerners as Crockett and Houston.

Newton Mallory Curtis' *The Hunted Chief: or, the Female Ranchero* (1847) was a Mexican War tale about the attempts of American soldiers to discover the place where Mexican rancheros are holding captive a band of Texas Rangers. When Harry Lee reports to his lieutenant that the rancheros have wiped out Bruxton's Rangers near Palo Alto, the officer exclaims: "It cannot be possible, or else the Mexicans were ten regiments strong! Bill and his Texans would whip two thousand Mexicans in a fair fight, any day."[23]

Texan character figures more forcefully in the same author's *The Prairie Guide: or the Rose of the Rio Grande* (1847). The early scenes of this book vaguely relate to Samuel Walker's scouting mission for General Taylor before the Battle of Palo

Alto in May, 1846. Taylor orders Fanchette, a Texan, to scout the territory between Fort Brown and Monterrey to determine the best approach for a battle. In disguise, Fanchette stops at the headquarters of Morales, a robber, who becomes suspicious of him and locks him in his house. The Texan falls in love with another prisoner, the beautiful Donna Isabella Xera. Eventually they escape together. A platoon of Mexican lancers overtakes them, and its leader shouts to the Texan: "Surrender, I say! Or I will order my men to charge upon you in an instant!"

"Never, by the eternal!" Fanchette cries. Cocking his pistol, he prepares to defend Isabella and himself.

"Ride him down!" shouts the leader of the Mexicans.

Pointing to the prostrate form of Isabella, Fanchette calls out, "Hell Hound! Would you trample down the innocent?"

"Ride him down!" repeats the Mexican.

On the cry of "Charge!" the Texan (for whom the story ends happily) begins firing, and, the author says, "In an instant, the sharp report startled the echoes of the ravine, then another, and another, and then riderless steeds wheeled from the ranks, and ran!"

Most of the characters in E. Z. C. Judson's *The Volunteer: or, the Maid of Monterey* (1847) are Kentuckians, although the Texas Rangers have prominent roles beside the Kentucky volunteers in the Battle of Monterrey. Judson stresses the famous feat of the Rangers and "the stalwart backwoodsmen" in breaking through the Monterrey houses.[24] The Texans and the Kentuckians fight side by side throughout the battle and are in all respects indistinguishable. Except for a few specific descriptions of the Texans themselves, *The Volunteer* was Judson's main word on the Typical Texan until after the Civil War when as "Ned Buntline" he specialized in Texan dime novels.

Texans figure by inference in Charles E. Averill's *Mexican Ranchero: or, the Maid of the Chapparal* (1847). A Yankee peddler, Sol Dalloby, had once narrowly escaped lynching at the hands of the Regulators. He was in the Regulators' bad graces because he had practiced some of those "famous little Yankee tricks which generally enable a down-east dealer to

make about a thousand percentum profit."[25] Smug though he
was about his ability to outwit them, he "respected"—and at a
distance—the physical might of the Texans in the Piney Woods.

In 1848 a Baltimore firm published *The Deaf Spy*, a posthu-
mous novel by James Wilmer Dallam, author of the above mentioned *The Lone Star*. It too was a tale "founded upon incidents
in the history of Texas." Though the truth of many of the events
in his story would be hard to prove, Dallam wrote so ably, compared to the average novelist treating a Texas subject, that his
book rings true. *The Deaf Spy* stars Deaf Smith, the famous
Texan scout, and his ward, Orin Hubbard, who seek revenge on
the Indians responsible for the murder of Smith's wife and Hubbard's parents. With his vast store of frontier knowledge and his
great dignity, Dallam's Smith could easily pass for one of Cooper's noble frontiersmen. Dallam, however, relates him to an
earlier time. Smith was so much like a gladiator or a "wrestler
of barbarian Rome" that "even the glance, which the comparison would direct to his iron-fisted hand, would be well satisfied
that its firm, compressing grip could easily start the warm blood,
gushing from the crushed finger or thumb on which his clasp
should fasten." His dress consisted of the loose garb of the frontier, and displayed his stalwart figure to the best advantage.[26]
The story centers on Smith's two-year imprisonment in Mexico
and Hubbard's acquaintance with a devotee of a fantastic, semi-
Christian cult whose members had settled on the Texas frontier.
Among paperbacks, *The Deaf Spy* is unique in its realistic description of living conditions and problems of the Texas settlers.
But like most of the novelettes, Dallam's book fosters the
idea that Texans were dauntless, able through courage and will
power to move mountains of Mexicans, savages, and other an-
noyances.

Henry William Herbert's *Pierre, the Partisan: a Tale of the
Mexican Marches* (1848) manages to treat Texan character
both romantically and realistically. Most of Herbert's popularity
was based on the sporting books he wrote as "Frank Forester,"
and his biographer, William Southworth Hunt, justifiably con-
demns *Pierre, the Partisan* as "hack work to cater to the Mexican

War interest."[27] Pierre is the most romantic character in any Texan narrative. His clothing was finely cut, he took solicitous care of his horse and equipment, and he carried rare and exotic foods on all his journeys. His "biscuits, and condiments, the leathern bottle, filled not with rum or whiskey but with fine Xeres wine, betokened tastes and habitudes more cultivated, perhaps manners more refined, than would ordinarily be expected from the rover of the Texan wilderness."[28]

Rudolph Valentino could have played Pierre. The "Partisan" is a complete gentleman, and he spends his time proving it by championing the rights and honor of the many defenseless women he meets. As a fighter he is blessed with uncommon intelligence; most of his triumphs result from his shrewdness and his ability to outsmart his enemies. If Herbert's readers long remembered Pierre for anything it was his personal charm and chivalry.

Pierre, the Partisan also features the Texas Rangers. While riding alone along the Rio Grande, Pierre is attracted to the headquarters of a Mexican ranch by the shrieks of women and the sound of violent fighting. Riding closer, he finds an enraged band of Texas Rangers wreaking mayhem on women and children, animals and ranch property. He commands the Rangers to stop their butchery, but they ignore him. Demanding to see their captain, he is told that they are all captains alike and that if he knows what is good for him he will ride on. When one of them approaches him menacingly, Pierre orders him to stand off; but the Ranger aims a blow at Pierre with his bowie knife, whereupon Pierre counters by shooting him through the head. A half-dozen Rangers then try to attack the Partisan, but not before his second pistol is out, and a second marauder lies stretched at his feet. "Then, at it we went, hand to hand."[29] Pierre at last re-establishes order at the ranch and saves the lives of the remaining women.

Later, during the height of the Mexican War, Pierre finds the ranch again under attack, this time by a company of Mexican soldiers. Pierre leads McCulloch's Texas Rangers against them. He suffers a fatal injury but, chivalrous to the last, lives long enough to receive assurances from the Rangers that they will escort the ladies to safety.

In *Pierre*, Herbert left the impression that some noble individuals at least were engaged in the strife on the southwestern frontier, and that chivalry, bravery, and love of justice were not unheard of as motives for some Texans' actions.

George Lippard, "unquestionably the most popular writer of the day,"[30] made a significant contribution to the spread of the notion about Texans in his novelette, *'Bel of Prairie Eden: a Romance of Mexico* (1848). Lippard was accustomed to writing books that went "off to the tune of twelve editions a year,"[31] and at the time of his *'Bel of Prairie Eden*'s appearance, the sale of Lippard's novels topped even that of foreigners in this country. Like most of his books *'Bel* was endowed with two qualities that spelled success: a sentimental love story and thrilling adventure in a distant region. It features the Texan efforts to block the Mexican advance toward San Antonio in 1842, and the suffering of a Texan family at the hands of Mexican rancheros. The book details the fantastic means which a son of the family employs to wreak vengeance on the rancheros' leader. The action is melodramatic and the plot is a needle in a haystack of pointless details, but Lippard's hero, John Grywin, was the Texan his readers were looking for. Aged twenty-one, he was a man of stalwart yet graceful proportions, with a face deeply tanned, strongly marked with aquiline features, and shadowed by dark hair and a beard. He was a magnificent horseman and a fearless hunter. As he mounted his horse, he slung his rifle, "Old King Death," over his shoulder. With his long hair floating in the wind, "and his eagle-like features, marked boldly out against the sky, he looked for all the world like a true knight of the chivalric age."[32]

John Hovey Robinson probably depended on the Crockett almanacs or the reports of travelers in writing his *The Lone Star: or, the Texan Bravo* (1852), which as we have noted appeared also in play form, and his *The Maid of the Ranche: or the Regulators and Moderators*. Robinson did not know Texans firsthand, and had traveled little, if any, in the West. In *The Lone Star*, the Texas Rangers, of the half-horse half-alligator school, preserve a nostalgic admiration for "Old Kentuck" while declaring their complete enthusiasm for their adopted country. Texas with its need of fighters furnished the chance the characters in this story wanted to put into use the fighting skill they had developed as Kentuckians. When Ethington, "the Texan Bravo," learns that the Mexicans are out especially to "get" him, he says, "Let them come—'The Texan Bravo' is ready; my life shall cost them a dozen of their best men"; and, he vows, "if they venture to close quarters, here are my pistols and bowie knife, ready to receive them; while my arms have the physical power of three such cowardly fellows."[33]

Robinson's *The Maid of the Ranche* is another story of the Regulators War. The last Texan paperback before the Civil War, it is compounded of all the elements encountered in most of the Texan novels. A thread of romance runs throughout and gives Robinson a chance to describe some of the Texans as chivalrous "knights of the forest." But the story emphasizes the backwoodsmen in the Piney Woods struggle. Both Meltiah Moss and Jack Lawless, "The Texan Cub," brag loudly in the Crockett manner. Lawless shouts: "I'm a heap of wild cats and other voracious varmints. I'm a Texan cub." And Moss echoes him: "Thar's a fight somewhar, an' I'm bound to go in for it! Hurra for Davie Crockett and the gouging system!" Part savage, part civilized, "The Texan Cub" was an object of terror, for he always carried a double barreled carbine, a brace of pistols, a bowie knife, and at least one hatchet.

The authors of the paperbacks were after nothing, artistic, political, or social, except the cash involved in selling a stirring tale. Like all writers with pots to boil, they wanted only to give the public what it wanted to buy. And the public that bought these books wanted a thrill on every page, an Indian or a Mexican behind every bush, and a hard-riding Texan hot on the trail of every one of them.

CHAPTER ELEVEN

Tall Texans, Short Stories, and Novels

THE same tastes that relished the novelettes welcomed a sizable shelf of novels and short stories featuring Texans. Whereas the writers of the paperbacks were willing enough to grind out anything that would sell, most of the authors who published full-length novels and collections of stories had their sights trained on quality. But artistic or not, it was the generous helpings of adventure that put these books across.

At least six collections of short stories about Texans appeared between the Mexican War and the Civil War. In looks, the first four resembled the paperbacks. The latter two came bound in boards.

In 1847 George Lippard compiled a fictionized account, *Legends of Mexico*, that dealt with the Mexican War battles in which Texans fought. Lippard had a sermon to preach in these stories, which were written in a style described by one critic as "high pressure, slightly elevated,"[1] and he was burning with zeal when he wrote them. He let Tom Paine speak for him on his title page: "We fight not to enslave, nor for conquest; but to make room upon the earth for honest men to live in." His stories develop the idea that the war was justifiable on every legal and moral ground. Of the reasons Lippard gave, practically all were Texan grievances against Mexico. He insisted that the Alamo cried for vengeance, and he heralded the war as a chance to right old wrongs and spread the blessings of American civilization across the hemisphere. "Does not the Almighty God lead the Nations to civilization through the reeking Golgothas of War?"[2]

Throughout Lippard's *Legends*, the Texans appear as little less than demigods. Speaking of Samuel Walker, Lippard pictures the fighter as "erect as an Indian, a fine specimen of an iron man,"[3] who with only ten hunters armed with rifles would be a match for at least a hundred disciplined soldiers. Ampudia, the Mexican general at Palo Alto, would do well, Lippard confided, to keep his men out of range of Captain Walker and "his iron-chested, death-eyed Texan rifles," for they had more than one record of blood to blot out and would waste no time in doing it.

Alfred W. Arrington, another author of the period, gained fame primarily as a novelist; but his group of sketches, *The Lives and Adventures of the Desperadoes of the Southwest* (1849), places him among the leading portrayers of Texan character. Arrington's "desperado" was not necessarily a criminal, but rather was any southwestern backwoodsman who took the law in his own hands whenever it seemed a good idea. Arrington left the impression that the "desperado" was the typical inhabitant of most Texas localities, an "eagle-man, whose soul takes delight in the gush of tempestuous, passionate excitement."[4] Only fighting men need fear him, however, for the stranger traveling on the frontier, unarmed, is as safe as if he were walking down Broadway or on Boston Common. But Arrington gave one word of warning to would-be visitors to Texas. He advised them to keep their unorthodox religious beliefs to themselves. When the question of religion came up in a certain drunken spree, one man who happened to be a deist said, according to report, that Jesus Christ was "a bastard." A Texan named Old Rose challenged him, and they fell to with their bowie knives. Arrington records that "the deist, for the improvement of his faith of the head, had his heart cut out!"[5]

The author John Tomlin came prepared. After visiting relatives in Texas in 1848, he returned to Ohio convinced that Texas was a dangerous, wholly fantastic place. Tomlin, a friend of Edgar Allan Poe, looked forward to a time when the South and West would produce a respectable literature of their own. In 1849 he published his *Tales of the Caddo*, which left nobody in doubt as to Texas' being a noteworthy place. Between the Sabine and Red rivers on a hot July day a norther blew in, Tomlin said, and within thirty minutes six out of a party of ten froze to death. Most of Tomlin's stories leave the impression that Texas, and East Texas in particular, was a region where only brawny men could survive. He supports his point by emphasizing the Regulators War and the prevalence of thievery. Tomlin's Ike Wayland, a character in "The Reformed Freebooter," tells his friend, Faraday of Georgia, that he is a fool to think he can survive in Texas without stealing. Ike Wayland was a muscular man with sinews of iron, who, "if he was born at all, must have been born in a pig-stye, cradled in a hog-trough, and fed on hickory nuts."[6]

Charles Wilkins Webber and Emerson Bennett were two writers who brought out substantial books of collected sketches. Both Webber's *Tales of the Southern Border* (1853) and Bennett's *Forest and Prairie: or, Life on the Frontier* (1860) emphasize the triumph of passion over law in early Texas. Webber's collection, a part of which appeared originally in periodicals, was immensely popular. One magazine found that these sketches appealed to readers because "they possess the merit of having for their subjects incidents strictly American."[7] Webber himself says he was so determined to become familiar with life in Texas that he traversed, alone, the greater part of it. The Texans in his sketches conform to the conception that was then growing in popularity, one reader calling them "bold, spirited portraits of character; salient, true to the borders."[8]

In Webber's adventure sketch, "Gonzaleze Again; or, the Bravo's Stratagem," a wealthy merchant offers a horse to "the Bravo" if he will lead a posse against a gang of thieves. The Texan is delighted. He wants the horse, of course, but he is also hankering for a little fun, since "he had not been in a single fight for a week or two; the Comanches had become distressingly shy, and the Mexicans so uncomfortably quiet, that he was almost bored to death by the vapid and tiresome monotony of peace."[9] Throughout his story the author makes it clear that Texans were men who could never be taken by surprise at anything. Their experience with every known peril had given them an air of coolness and indifference, as if danger, no matter how great, was something "to be expected, and certainly not wondered at."[10]

Bennett's collection, *Forest and Prairie: or, Life on the Frontier,* includes the story, "Colonel Bowie of Arkansas." Riding toward San Antonio, the Alamo martyr, Jim Bowie, who gave his name to the bowie knife, stops at a stream to water his horse. A shot startles him, and the bullet whistles past his head. Perplexed, he remounts and heads quickly for cover. He spends the night in a deserted cabin and is about to ride on the next morning when two strangers approach the house. They discover his horse before Bowie can prevent their doing so, but he is able to conceal himself. In his hiding, Bowie learns from their talk that they were party to the shooting the day before. They enter the house looking for him.

In a tone that seems to freeze their blood, Bowie says, "Here!" and the two behold him standing in the doorway, with a rifle "brought to a deadly aim."[11]

Bowie forces them to tell who shot at him. The man named Joe confesses but begs Bowie to spare his life. Bowie shoots him through the head. The other, Bill Harvey of Arkansas, pleads for his life because he has a wife and child. Since Bowie has heard of him, he agrees to let him fight for his life, with knives. In the fight, Bowie stabs Harvey; and as Harvey is breathing his last, his antagonist identifies himself as "Colonel James Bowie of Arkansas."

"Rather say the devil!" groans Harvey. "Ef I'd a know'd your name before, I'd been better prepared for the fight. You've killed me and may my curse go with you!"

Bowie walks quietly away, mounts his horse, and rides off in colossal unconcern, leaving the bodies where they fell.[12]

The longer fictions about Texans were efforts to improve on the materials which had been cheapened in the novelettes. Their authors partly succeeded in writing a respectable literature, but domestic law and order figure as little in these works as they do in the paperbacks. These books emphasized the chaotic conditions on the frontier and featured, for the most part, the brave Texan fighters who managed to battle their way through.

Though all these works were fiction, they were not all novels, for some of them have only the sketchiest of plots. This is true of *Col. Crockett's Exploits and Adventures in Texas* (1836), which purports to be fact, but is not. Others, such as Emerson Bennett's *Clara Moreland; or Adventures in the Far South-west,* are true novels.

Col. Crockett's Exploits and Adventures in Texas tells the story of Davy's trip from Tennessee through Arkansas to his death at the Alamo. The book says little about Texan character, but it suggests much by showing Crockett's enthusiasm for the Texan cause and the eagerness of the Texans to make him one of them. Though it carried the by-line "Written by Himself," *Exploits and Adventures* was the work of a ghost writer, Richard Penn Smith, who turned it out immediately after the news of Crockett's death reached Philadelphia. Smith had never been to Texas, but before he set to work he read all the books on Texas available.[13] Within a year after its publication the book sold ten thousand copies, and the sales remained steady for quite some time, a biographer of Smith reporting in 1849 that few books had gained an equal popularity.[14]

In Smith's book Crockett, heading west through Nacogdoches, boasts: "I will die with my Betsey in my arms. No, I will not die—I'll grin down the walls of the Alamo, and the Americans will lick up the Mexicans like fine salt."[15] The book ends at a time shortly before the Mexicans proved how mistaken he was.

Smith, it is clear, was well acquainted with Crockett's national reputation. His book is wholly concerned with the mythical being who existed only in the popular imagination. A review of the volume paid tribute to "the true David Crockett, who is an ideal, not an actual man. His private qualities are forgotten and merged in those of his class and age—of whom he is the allegory and personification."[16] The brave men who fought beside Crockett were largely ignored in *Exploits and Adventures,* but the book furnished one of the earliest descriptions of Texans as the hot-blooded kin of all Kentuckians.

The book which announced itself as the first Texas novel was *Mexico Versus Texas* (1838).[17] One Anthony Ganilh is commonly supposed to be its author, though a second edition, entitled *Ambrosio de Letinez,* bears the name of A. T. Myrthe. Whoever wrote it, this work is historically significant as an early literary treatment of Texan character. Santa Anna, says Ganilh, was foolhardy in maintaining the notion that the Texans were inferior in bravery to the soldiers in his own command. "After having seen a thousand of his soldiers killed, at the storming of Bejar, by two hundred backwoodsmen," Santa Anna, in Ganilh's estimation, was ridiculous to rush with his soldiers into "the very snare prepared for him; and the fatal twenty-first of April [at San Jacinto] taught him the difference between the two races."[18] It was no wonder that the Mexicans, according to Ganilh, considered the Texans "monsters in human form, worse, if possible, than cannibals."[19]

It remained for a writer of the Old World to catch fully the spirit of adventure on the southwestern frontier of the United States. Charles Sealsfield, the Austrian novelist, made two pronouncements on Texan character that sold widely in America. They were *The Cabin Book, or Sketches of Life in Texas* and the long story, "The Squatter Chief, or the First American in Texas." Sealsfield won the praise of a growing public as well as the acclaim of Longfellow, who thought his descriptions of the Southwest "striking."[20] The *Knickerbocker Magazine* extolled him as having come closer, perhaps, to a literary expression of the American spirit than any other contemporary novelist.[21] Sealsfield did know American character. His knowledge of it led him to criticize Cooper, for "in the entire United States you will not find dolts who permit themselves to be pulled about like Leatherstocking, nor a Kentuckian who would stand before a captain with his cap in his hand, as is the case in The Prairie."[22] Both *The Cabin Book* and "The Squatter Chief" are lucid pictures of the settling of Texas.

The Cabin Book, or Sketches of Life in Texas, usually considered Sealsfield's best work, is arranged as a discussion of the

wisdom of annexing Texas. One speaker asks: "Will you willingly tie yourself to a fresh swarm of exiles, gamblers, murderers and lawless rabble?"[23]

Colonel Morse, from Texas, confesses that the new country
has indeed "rabble in abundance; adventurers of all kinds, exiles, gamblers, murderers," and yet, he says, "not too many! . . .
This rabble was of great service to us, perhaps more so than your
quiet, peaceful, respectable citizens would have been"[24] in fighting Mexico.

"The Squatter Chief" centers on the experiences of two enterprising Kentucky families who settled near San Antonio on
land which the Mexican government granted them for their
help in "one of the Mexican revolutions." The two families and
the many settlers who joined them are typical Kentucky fighters and hunters, all of whom become good Texans and are proud
of it.

Charles Wilkins Webber wrote, besides the tales mentioned
earlier, three long works of fiction about Texans: *Old Hicks the
Guide, or, Adventures in the Camanche Country in Search of
a Gold Mine* (1848), its sequel, *The Gold Mines of the Gila*
(1849), and *The Prairie Scout, or Agatone the Renegade*
(1852). The *Spirit of the Times* greeted *Old Hicks the Guide* as
the work of a "resolute, active, and fearless" Texas Ranger,
"with about as much regard for human life as a butcher has for a
bullock, yet possessed of a certain rude chivalry, that qualifies
our natural abhorrence of the man of blood."[25] *Graham's* liked
it better—in fact, much better, since this work was preferred to
a couple of novels by Herman Melville: "Mr. Webber's book
is one of the most captivating of its kind ever produced in the
United States. . . . It evinces more genius than *Typee* or *Omoo*."[26]

Though posterity has not agreed with the enthusiastic editor
of *Graham's*, *Old Hicks* is indeed one of the most agreeable
books ever written about the Texas frontier. It compares well in
style with Francis Parkman's *Oregon Trail* and has much of that
book's authenticity. Webber's story relates the adventures of a
gold expedition traversing the Texas Panhandle escorted by a
company of Texas Rangers. The Rangers are men who never

turn back—"at least before they have tested whether there be really such a word as impossible necessary to their vocabulary."[27] Of the average Texan frontiersman, Webber wrote that he "is always ready, if you give him plenty of ammunition, to go wherever his horse is able to carry him. He certainly, of all men, most religiously observes the biblical precept, 'think not of what ye shall eat or what ye shall wear for the morrow.' "[28]

The Prairie Scout, or Agatone the Renegade fictionized Webber's own early days in Texas. When Webber, newly arrived from Kentucky, joins his friend, Big Bill P., he learns from Big Bill that he must get over his greenness as soon as possible, that life in Texas is all fighting—usually with Indians, sometimes with Mexicans, and often with outlaws. "We call it good shooting," says Bill, "when they don't even kick."[29] Of Texas, Bill declares that they "give you man's meat here; rough country, rough doings, but it does make men!"[30] After Webber had been in Texas for some time, he recommended that a Mexican prisoner about to be hanged should be tied to a log and thrown into the river instead. Bill rejoiced that he was now "becoming worthy of Texas."[31] The Rangers under the command of Jack Hays ride dramatically into later sections of the book; they are physical giants, rough, and mostly "from the south-western States, with the true Kentucky half-horse half-alligator profile, and the usual allowance of thunder, lightning, and earthquake."[32]

The Gold Mines of the Gila describes a brave but ragtag band of Texans advancing in a "retaliatory invasion" against Mexico. Their tatterdemalion ranks mixed together every breed of tough and vicious men, "black-browed cut-throats," "ruffianly cowboys," "stalwart hunters," "small farmers," and a "ferocious phalanx" of captains, colonels, majors, and generals, with scarcely as many men apiece to command "as they have each and individually eaten in their day—mixed up with young adventurers of all sorts and every country." Some few buckskinned Rangers went with them. They were "armed to the teeth," and stepped "about like lords of the soil."[33]

Among other things, Samuel Hammett's *A Stray Yankee in Texas* (1853) describes the efforts of a Yankee to cope with

Texas and the Texans, and presents Hammett's opinions of the
Regulars and Moderators. The book proved popular enough to
go through two editions in the first six months after its publication. Hammett reported that in Harrison County there was a
stream that was called Widow's Creek because within a distance
of five miles resided twenty-five widows whose husbands had
met death in the fighting between the two factions. Hammett
strove in his book to "give a correct idea of scenes and scenery,
men and manners, as they exist in a section of our country of
which much has been written but little is really known."[34] His
writing surely did nothing to improve the reputation of Texans.
After reading *A Stray Yankee in Texas*, only the breed of people
who willingly flirt with danger would have dared to go there.
Hammett compared gigantic Texas to the Texans themselves.
The storms were hurricanes, the rivers vast inland seas; where
everything else was expanded, it did not surprise Hammett
to find that man himself was expansive.[35] The Texans' virtues,
their courage, their hospitality, their crimes, and their size were
all gargantuan.

The suggestion of danger in Texas comes out even in Hammett's understatement. Visiting in Marshall, Texas, Hammett
met a peaceable looking old man "with no implements of war
visible, except a double-barrel and a bowie-knife." The loafers
in town remarked, laconically, that *he* was mighty poorly provided for and "wouldn't stand more than half a chance" if somebody took offense at him.[36]

Emerson Bennett's two romantic novels, *Clara Moreland; or,
Adventures in the Far South-west* (1853) and *Viola* (1854),
concern the love affair of Henry Walton, a Virginian, and Clara
Moreland, niece of an emigrant Kentuckian. The plots of both
novels consist of the narrow escapes of the main characters in
their encounters with Indians and Mexicans. In both novels
Texas is pictured as the reservoir of the nation's bravest men,
the true home of matchless fighters. In *Clara Moreland* it is only
natural that the Texas Rangers under Samuel Walker should
become the heroic deliverers of Clara and her father from their
Mexican captors.

Today nobody knows more than the dim outlines of the Texas career of Jeremiah Clemens, who wrote two Texan novels, *Bernard Lile; an Historical Romance* (1856) and *Mustang Gray; a Romance* (1858). In his day Clemens was an indefatigable traveler, author, and soldier. He says in *Bernard Lile* that he visited every place described in the novel. He survived rough times on the Texas frontier and fought in the Mexican War. Both of his novels are unmistakably the work of a writer who knew his locale as well as his trade. *Bernard Lile* recounts the full-blown career of a world traveler who decided to go to Texas to aid in the Revolution. He arrives just in time to join Milam's attack on San Antonio. While storming the town, Lile shows the Texans a smart trick: breaking through the walls of the houses. Milam says to his men: "Remember that trick, boys; it may help us at a pinch another day."[37] Then the story goes on to show how they later put Lile's trick to good use in Monterrey. Lile would have been one of the martyrs remaining in the Alamo if he had not volunteered to carry a message to Houston. David Crockett started to volunteer for the mission himself, but as he says to Colonel Travis: "When I was in Congress, I noticed that all the fellows were striving for glory; but talking wasn't one of my gifts, and precious little glory fell to my lot." Here in Texas, Crockett says, "I'm arter glory, Colonel Travis, mixed up with a sprinkling of Mexican hide and tallow. I reckon these boys are much of my way of thinking; and if you ain't got no objection we'll just stay where we are."[38]

Jeremiah Clemens' *Mustang Gray* is a fictionized biography of one of the more famous Texas Rangers in the Mexican War, a man whom Clemens knew personally. *Russell's Magazine*, while acknowledging that the hero Gray's brave exploits naturally excite the reader's imagination, remarked that "we cannot conceal from ourselves the fact that he is very decidedly a desperado, and not a little of a blackguard."[39] During the war, the actual Gray was first attached as a lieutenant to a company of Texas Mounted Volunteers, or Rangers. Later he commanded a company of his own, the "Mustangers" or the "Mustang Grays." *Russell's* probably referred to the actions of the group which "at times outraged the sensibilities and the code of civilized warfare cherished by American soldiers not of their background"[40]—in other words, American soldiers who believed in giving the Mexicans at least a fighting chance.

The Rangers under Gray were ready for anything that gave them "present employment, and promised future remuneration." According to Clemens, their excessive brutality to the Mexicans is understandable when one remembers how much the Texans suffered from the Mexicans during and after the Texas Revolution. In retaliation for the loss of two Rangers killed in capturing a Mexican ranch, Gray orders the owner and a priest to be tied and burned in the house. Whenever prisoners were turned over to him for protection during the Monterrey campaign, they all died immediately. It was no wonder that the mere mention of his name was enough to scare the wits out of most Indians and Mexicans.

Two books that emphasized the deep contrasts between Yankee and Texan characteristics were Alfred W. Arrington's *The Rangers and Regulators of the Tanaha: or, Life Among the Lawless* (1856) and Samuel Hammett's *Piney Woods Tavern: or, Sam Slick in Texas* (1858). Arrington was a friend of Seba Smith, the creator of "Major Jack Downing," the famous typical Yankee; and Arrington may have been attempting to typify the Texan as effectively in his *The Rangers and Regulators*. Here the Yankee peddler, Jonathan, had been persuaded to go after the likely market among the settlers in Texas; but after realizing that he was to be exposed constantly to grave dangers, he wished he "wur back again in Vermont, they have no such doin's there."[41]

Seen through the Yankee's eyes, the wild goings-on in Shelby County seem more fearful than they do in any other fiction work. Arrington realized that his character would be charged with an excess of "dark and gloomy coloring." But he insisted that he included only facts. Four separate warring factions people his book: a robber gang kidnapping slaves in the United States, the lynchers who oppose the robbers, the lawless Regulators in Shelby County, and the rip-roaring Rangers under Sam Houston who eventually set things straight.

Sam Houston is the most impressive Texan in either *Piney Woods Tavern* or *The Rangers and Regulators*. In Hammett's book, when Houston discovered that the buckskin breeches he had ordered from a little Dutch tailor were too small, he became so enraged that the tailor, in fear of his life, left town forever. In Arrington's book, when one of the Regulators asks Sam's opinion of them, Houston spits a mouthful of tobacco in his eye.

"Why didn't you knock him down?" asks one of the outlaws.

"If any pusson wishes old Sam knocked down," the victim replies, "he's welcome to try the speriment hisself; fur, by thunder! this here chile don't want to risk it."[42]

When one considers the historical significance of the fiction in which America first met the Typical Texan, he can forget its shortcomings as art. In spite of their good intentions, not one of the writers who dealt with Texans wrote a wholly memorable book. Somehow their words lacked the spark that would keep them alive. And it takes a pretty alert librarian to find their books today. The character traits, on the other hand, that interested these men have by no means passed out of America's concern. These writers were literary trail-breakers, picking their way through canyons, around boulders, and over passes in territory that every generation since their time has been glad they bothered to explore. Though they gave us no enduring classic, they gave us something more, for they originated one of this country's few contributions to world letters, the western story.

The Texan on horseback sits today as firmly and as tall in the literary saddle as he ever did. An immortal novel may yet be written about him. But the Texan in fiction has already achieved immortality. For a century he has chased the same Indians, talked the same lusty lingo, fired the same six-guns, and played the same chivalrous role with the women as he did in the earliest tales that featured him. In the hundreds of "new" western stories appearing every year, his world and his ways live on.

CHAPTER TWELVE

Round-Up

A WESTERN WOMAN once remarked to an educator, "Nothing good ever came out of the East." The teacher slyly responded, "Not even the westerners?"[1] His reply probably left the woman as astonished—and as wordless—as many present Americans are when they learn the true origin of the Typical Texan.

Where did the Typical Texan come from? It is pretty clear that he originated outside Texas.

Throughout the years that have passed since the Typical Texan took shape in the minds of the world, the native sons of America's big state have worked hard and faithfully to keep their legendary representative in his prime. The nation as a whole has always had plenty of reason to know that Texans are proud of the Typical Texan. Their willingness to play up to the role makes that obvious. Each year a sizable portion of the world's non-Texans become more aware of the fabled being whom loyal Texans love so well. The men of the Lone Star were perhaps never more happy to sponsor the popular notion of Texans than they were as fighters in World War II; and the years since V-J Day have shown no decline in their enthusiasm for "God's country."

If outsiders often find the Texan's boisterous behavior and his undying pride in his heritage wearying, they have only themselves to blame. They and their forebears since Texas first welcomed American emigrants are responsible for the character who has for a century epitomized Texans to the world. Their zeal, as much as the Texans', makes the Typical Texan today as lively as he was in the golden age of the 1830's and 1840's when Texans were fending off Indians with one hand and brushing aside Mexicans with the other. Few people, Texan or otherwise, seem eager to forget him.

The truth is, of course, that publishers, dramatists, travelers, and the tellers of tales in the American East should receive most of the credit for making the Typical Texan the ageless phenomenon that he seems to be. As real people, Crockett and Houston and various Rangers made a deep and abiding impression on all who saw them, independent of the effect intended by the professional image-makers who glamorized and glorified them. But the individuality and "color" of a large portion of the people who settled beyond the Sabine were only an indirect influence in the birth of the public notion about them. The process that fashioned the Typical Texan, the most enduring character type America has yet produced, went on for the most part without the assistance of Texans themselves. Writers and actors and paid funny men spread a special idea of Texans in many areas where it might not have gone. These men and women were big agents in popularizing the mythical man of the Southwest. It was their suggestions that stimulated the public's creation of a bragging, fighting, cavorting big fellow to typify all Texans.

Why did non-Texans create the Typical Texan? And why has he endured?

Since the distant decades before the states split apart over differences in their basic governmental principles, America's taste in the arts and her attitudes toward life in general have been colored with romance. To many of her most devoted citizens, America's recent maturity as a nation has been disappointing; to them it was a pity that she had to grow up at all. Such people are the spiritual kin of the thousands of nineteenth-century Americans whose imaginations tingled whenever the West was mentioned. Theirs is the spirit today that wishes we still had a vast empty territory on the sundown side of the Mississippi that could forever remain free of the plow and the fence and the filling station. In their estimation, one of the saddest dates in American history is 1890, when the government officially declared that the last frontier was gone.

The nostalgic public who accepted that sober geographic fact made no room for it in their hearts. No law required it, and nothing else brought it about. It is not easy to forget the high excitement that prevailed on the frontier when men were men, and man the individual still seemed to hold firmly the reins of his own destiny.

As the wilderness of the Great Plains and Texas steadily receded before the onslaughts of white families making homes, a vast public grew increasingly hungry to feed its imagination on depictions of the frontier world and its way of life that was soon to pass. Consequently, the final decades of the nineteenth century saw an eagerness for stories of the aging West that surpassed anything this country experienced before the Civil War, and the 1880's and '90's were the great years of the "Wild West" shows starring Buffalo Bill and Texas Jack. During these years, too, dime novels reached their highest popularity. In these latter-day novelettes, the western American, who either was an actual Texan or resembled one, entered his heyday, and in the many western story magazines of the present he has remained there.

The weekly crowds that stampede the Saturday afternoon western movies are similar to the group that made the western magazine popular. Hollywood, one of the greatest impression-makers of the present century, has long fed its public a diet composed largely of glamour. It has filled the screen and the popular imagination with two purely American culture symbols: the movie queen and the cowboy. The appeal of both is completely romantic. Ever since the days of William S. Hart and Tom Mix, the marquees have always carried some cowboy hero's name in lights. The pictures that star the cowboy are usually pretty thin stuff meant to appeal only to children and adventure fans innocent of high artistic standards. But year by year the list grows longer of pictures set in the West of the last century that reach heights of artistic excellence and that are superb entertainment as well. Critic and public alike acclaimed *Stagecoach, The Westerner, Red River,* and *The Gunfighter.* The judges liked them because they were top-quality dramas, intelligently made. Whether it knew it or not, the public as a group liked them because they revitalized a world and a way of life that has had a fundamental appeal since Americans were first stirred by the fascinating call of the West.

Radio stories and serials follow the same pattern with Roy Rogers, Hopalong Cassidy, and Gene Autry. And such men, with their Stetsons and their pistols and their spurs, clank around as the great heroes of television. The technological world of TV and the dusty sagebrush realm of cowboys and Indians are not so far apart as they might logically seem.

Today, with the American nation composed of 150,000,000 people settled over a conquered area spanning a continent from sea to sea, it is difficult to speak with assurance about such a nebulous matter as "the American Dream." Certainly the term itself is much too big and much too vague to pin down to everyone's satisfaction. But it is safe to say that the adventurous life of the mounted American frontiersman embodies that dream for many people. Here in the middle years of the twentieth century the comforts and luxuries of settled society somehow fail to seem so wonderful when one recalls the shining excitements, the challenges, and even the perils, all now vanished, that only a few decades ago were the proud inheritance of every young American who wished to claim them for his own. Never before or since has the individual mattered so much as he did during the years when he was wresting Texas and the trans-Mississippi West from its primeval owners. Never before or since has so much promise beckoned to him. This nation has always admired the "red-blooded American." There was never a home more fit for him than the West of the nineteenth century. It was a man's world, and man was abundantly free to make the most of it.

Tex is certainly "red-blooded." The public that devours the "pulps" and clutches the arms of its seats as a Texan on horseback hurtles across the screen after the dirty rustlers is only a part of the group that believes in the Typical Texan—believes in him and encourages flesh and blood Texans to act like him. Unnumbered other Americans who pride themselves on being consistently realistic thinkers admit to an exception when it comes to the western man in the saddle. Though they steer clear of "trash" literature and the formula-born "horse-operas" of Hollywood, they take the Texan Tradition as fable based on fact, and are supremely glad.

The Typical Texan has been cavorting around now for more than a hundred years, telling his windies, charming the ladies, and fanning his pistols at come-what-may. Though he has never thought of himself in so sober a role, he has long filled a need deep in the hearts of all citizens of democracies. That is the need to feel that somewhere there exist the freedom and limitless opportunity which characterized the period of the last American frontier. Then and there man could seek and find the pot of gold at the foot of every rainbow; there the fulfilment of his dreams was limited only by the capacities within himself. This is the democratic ideal.

As long as it remains so, Americans will continue to be stirred by the tradition of the forthright, the courageous, the free—the Typical Texan.

Notes

Bibliography

Index

NOTES

Introduction

1. I am indebted to Professor Edward Everett Dale of the University of Oklahoma for "The Wild Cowhand."

2. *Sketches from "Texas Siftings"* (New York, 1882), p. 106.

3. *Houston Telegraph and Texas Register,* August 28, 1839.

4. Mrs. Viele, *"Following the Drum": A Glimpse of Frontier Life* (New York, 1858), p. 152.

5. *El Paso Herald-Post,* June 24, 1950.

Chapter One

1. Quoted in Allan Nevins, *American Social History as Recorded by British Travellers* (New York, 1924), pp. 183-84.

2. "American Humor," *United States Magazine and Democratic Review,* XVII (September, 1845), 215.

3. Timothy Flint, *Recollections of the Last Ten Years* (Boston, 1826), p. 7.

4. Wilson Flagg, *The Tailor's Shop* (Boston, 1844), p. 47.

5. Quoted in Richard M. Dorson, *Davy Crockett: American Comic Legend* (New York, 1939), p. 126.

6. *The Life and Adventures of Wm. Harvard Stinchfield* (Portland, Maine, 1851), p. 23.

7. Lady Emmeline Wortley, *Travels in the United States* (New York, 1851), p. 73.

8. Haliburton, *The Clockmaker* (New York, 1843), p. 80.

9. Harry Halyard, *The Ocean Monarch* (Boston, 1848), p. 93.

10. *Crockett's Yaller Flower Almanac* (New York, 1836), p. 13.

11. *Nature and Human Nature* (New York, 1855), p. 18.

12. "Writers of the Western Country," *Western Monthly Review,* II (June, 1828), 13.

13. Flint, *op. cit.,* p. 73.

14. *Ibid.,* p. 63.

15. Henry Nash Smith, *Virgin Land* (Cambridge, Mass., 1950), p. 54, quoting *Niles Register,* XXIV (May 17, 1823), 166.

16. J. M. Peck, *A New Guide for Emigrants to the West* (Boston, 1837), p. 124.

17. *Nick of the Woods: or the Jibbenainosay* (Philadelphia, 1837). The passage is quoted from Mark Van Doren's edition (New York, 1928), p. 49.

18. "The Kentuckian in New York," *Western Monthly Review,* I (June, 1827), 88.

19. *Domestic Manners of the Americans* (New York, 1832), p. 36.

20. J. S. Robb, *Streaks of Squatter Life* (Philadelphia, 1847), p. 71.

21. *Crockett's Yaller Flower Almanac* (New York, 1836), p. 19.

22. *Western Monthly Magazine,* V (October, 1836), 626.

23. Quoted in Julius W. Pratt, *Expansionists of 1812,* p. 40.

24. "The East and the West," an anonymous article in *United States Magazine and Democratic Review,* XXII (May, 1848), 402.

25. *An Account of Col. Crockett's Tour to the North and Down East,* p. 65.

26. Quoted in V. L. O. Chittick, *Ring-Tailed Roarers,* p. 24.

27. Christopher Clodpole, *The Clodpole Papers* (1844), p. 11.

Chapter Two

1. See Ralph H. Gabriel, *The Course of American Democratic Thought, an Intellectual History Since 1815* (New York, 1940), chap. VIII.

2. Baldwin, *The Flush Times of Alabama and Mississippi* (New York, 1853), p. 73.

3. *Crockett Almanac, Containing Life, Manners, and Adventures* etc. (New York, 1854), no page.

4. *New York Spirit of the Times,* February 17, 1838.

5. Quoted by James Hall, *Western Monthly Magazine*, II, 660.

6. Quoted in Sir Charles Lyell, *A Second Visit to the United States of North America* (London, 1850), I, 128.

7. Frances Trollope, *Domestic Manners of the Americans* (NewYork, 1832), p.35.

8. *The Squatter's Almanac* (New York and Philadelphia, 1845), no page.

9. *Ibid.*

10. *Ibid.*

11. *Ibid.*

12. *Crockett Almanac* (Boston, 1849), quoted in Dorson, *Davy Crockett*, p. 108.

13. *Travels in the United States* (New York, 1851), p. 162. -

Chapter Three

1. *Houston Telegraph and Texas Register*, July 24, 1839.

2. Eugene C. Barker, *The Life of Stephen F. Austin: Founder of Texas* (Nashville, Tennessee, 1925), p. 149.

3. Quoted in *Niles Register*, XXXIX (November 6, 1830), 173.

4. [Lawrence], *Texas in 1840, or the Emigrant's Guide to the New Republic; Being the Result of Observation, Enquiry and Travel in That Beautiful Country* (New York, 1840), p. 229.

5. Page, *Prairiedom: Rambles and Scrambles in Texas or New Estremadura* (New York, 1845), p. 66.

6. For an authoritative discussion of the impact of the West on American thought see Henry Nash Smith, *op. cit.*

7. *The American Character* (New York, 1944), p. 8.

8. From his poem, "America Was Promises."

9. Alfred W. Arrington, *The Lives and Adventures of the Desperadoes of the Southwest* (New York, 1849), p. 49.

10. *Holden's Dollar Magazine*, I (April, 1848), 308.

11. In his 1844 campaign paper, the *Clay Tribune*.

12. *G. T. T.: or, the Wonderful Adventures of a Pullman* (Boston, 1877), p. vi.

13. *Ibid.*, p. v.

14. Barker, *The Life of Stephen F. Austin*, p. 152.

15. Pattie, *The Personal Narrative of James O. Pattie, of Kentucky*, ed. by Timothy Flint (Cincinnati, 1833), p. 289.

16. Quoted in Marquis James, *The Raven* (Indianapolis, 1929), p. 197.

17. *Sketches from "Texas Siftings,"* p. 151.

18. *Western Monthly Magazine*, II (October, 1834), 667.

19. Baldwin, *The Flush Times of Alabama and Mississippi* (New York, 1853), p. 224.

20. Philip Hone, *The Diary of Philip Hone, 1828-1851*, ed. by Allan Nevins, 2 vols. (New York, 1927), II, 744.

21. *Ibid.*, p. 692.

22. Clarence Wharton, *San Jacinto, the Sixteenth Decisive Battle* (Newark, New Jersey, 1930), p. 59.

23. *Western Monthly Magazine*, V (April, 1836), 232.

24. *A Letter to the Hon. Henry Clay, on the Annexation of Texas to the United States* (Boston, 1837), p. 20.

25. *Clay Tribune*, November 2, 1844.

26. James, *The Raven*, p. 271.

27. *Texas and the Texans* (Philadelphia, 1841), II, 17.

28. *New York Herald*, May 24, 1836.

29. John E. Roller, "Captain John Sowers Brooks," *Texas Historical Association Quarterly*, IX (January, 1906), 163.

30. *New York Spirit of the Times*, July 16, 1836.

31. *New York Herald*, May 27, 1836.

32. C. Edwards Lester, *Sam Houston and His Republic* (New York, 1846), p. 7.

Chapter Four

1. *New York Sun,* December 29, 1838.

2. *Knickerbocker,* XXV (May, 1845), 386.

3. To distinguish between Crockett the man and Crockett the folk hero in this book, I refer to the former as "David," to the latter as "Davy." Works of "Crockett" which I cite often are ghost-written. While many "Crockett" writings are known to be spurious, they all have a flavor which, if not authentic to the man, is compatible to his tradition. Constance Rourke in her *Davy Crockett* (New York, 1934) discusses the authorship of the Crockett books.

4. Rourke, *op. cit.,* p. 128.

5. Even though, according to Ralph L. Rusk in *The Literature of the Middle Western Frontier* (New York, 1925), I, 420, such plays as *The Lion of the West* and the dramatized version of R. M. Bird's *Nick of the Woods* were anything but popular with audiences composed of actual westerners.

6. *New York Traveller, Spirit of the Times and Family Journal,* December 21, 1833.

7. Walter M. Leman, *Memories of an Old Actor* (San Francisco, 1886), p. 159.

8. *Spirit of the Times,* February 2, 1842.

9. Ludlow, *Dramatic Life as I Found It* (St. Louis, 1880), p. 170.

10. James, *The Raven,* p. 133.

11. Lester, *Sam Houston,* p. 54.

12. James, *op. cit.,* p. 366.

13. *Ibid.,* p. 359.

14. Quoted in the *Telegraph and Texas Register,* March 21, 1837.

15. *New York Herald,* June 9, 1836.

16. *Ibid.,* June 10, 1836.

17. Houston, *Speeches of Sam Houston, of Texas, In Reference to the Military Occupation of Santa Fe, and in Defence of Texas and the Texian Volunteers in the Mexican War* (delivered in the Senate of the United States, June 29 and July 3, 1850), p. 3.

18. Col. Edward Stiff, *The Texan Emigrant: Being a Narration of the Adventures of the Author in Texas* (Cincinnati, 1840), p. 34.

19. John C. Duval, *The Adventures of Big-Foot Wallace,* quoted in B. A. Botkin, *A Treasury of American Folklore* (New York, 1944), p. 158.

20. Duval, *The Adventures of Big-Foot Wallace* (Macon, Georgia, 1870), p. 285.

21. *Ibid.,* p. 292.

22. *Ibid.,* p. 294.

23. *Ibid.,* p. 293.

24. *Ibid.,* pp. 293-94.

25. *Ibid.,* p. 295.

26. *Ibid.,* p. 298.

27. *Ibid.,* p. 299.

Chapter Five

1. Nelson Lee, *Three Years Among the Camanches* (Albany, New York, 1859), p. 32.

2. Samuel C. Reid, Jr., *The Scouting Expeditions of McCulloch's Texas Rangers* (Philadelphia, 1847), p. 23.

3. Constance Rourke, *American Humor, a Study of the National Character* (New York, 1931), p. 52.

4. Charles Averill, *Kit Carson, the Prince of the Gold Hunters; or, the Adventurers of the Sacramento* (Boston, 1849), pp. 57-58, quoted in Henry Nash Smith, *Virgin Land,* p. 89.

5. Quoted in the *New York Herald,* June 15, 1836.

6. *New York Sunday Morning News,* December 27, 1835.

7. *New York Sun,* December 8, 1846.

8. *Spirit of the Times,* December 19, 1846.

9. *Pennsylvanian,* June 15, 1847.

10. "Song of Myself," Section 34.

11. Frederick Law Olmsted, *A Journey Through Texas; or, a Saddle-trip on the Southwestern Frontier* (New York, 1857), p. 300.

12. Walter Prescott Webb, *The Texas Rangers; a Century of Frontier Defense* (Boston, 1935), p. 93.

13. *Graham's Magazine,* XXXVI (February, 1850), 134.

14. *Niles Weekly Register*, LXXIII (October 23, 1847), 115.

15. *Sketches of the Campaign in Northern Mexico*, footnote on p. 97.

16. Webb, *op. cit.*, p. 118, quoting A. G. Brackett's *Lane's Brigade*, pp. 173-74.

17. Olmsted, *op. cit.*, p. 302.

18. *Loc. cit.*

19. T. B. Thorpe, *Our Army at Monterey* (Philadelphia, 1847), p. 77.

20. [William Walton], *Thrilling Incidents of the Wars of the United States* (Philadelphia, 1848), p. 565.

21. Reid, *op. cit.*, p. 192.

22. Webb, *op. cit.*, p. 110.

23. Quoted in the *Spirit of the Times*, February 26, 1848.

24. Quoted in Webb, *op. cit.*, p. 119.

25. *New Orleans Bulletin*, June 6, 1836, quoted in *New York Times*, June 22, 1836.

26. An anonymous letter from Buena Vista, Mexico, quoted in the *Washington National Intelligencer* and requoted in *Niles Weekly Register*, LXXIII (October 23, 1847), 115.

27. *New Orleans Delta*, quoted in the *Flag of Our Union*, February 5, 1848.

28. *Sketches of the Campaign in Northern Mexico*, "By an Officer" (New York, 1853), p. 97.

29. Quoted in Donald Day, "Leaves of Mesquite Grass," in Boatright and Day, *From Hell to Breakfast* (Dallas, 1944), p. 74.

Chapter Six

1. Walter Blair, *Native American Humor 1800-1900* (New York, 1937), p. 3.

2. Van Wyck Brooks, *The World of Washington Irving* (New York, 1944), p. 383.

3. *Western Monthly Magazine*, V (October, 1836), 626.

4. Julius Froebel, *Seven Years' Travel in Central America, Northern Mexico, and the Far West of the United States* (London, 1859), p. 446.

5. N. Doran Maillard, *The History of the Republic of Texas* (London, 1842), p. 212.

6. *Ibid.*, p. 626.

7. Webb, *op. cit.*, p. x.

8. Arthur M. Schlesinger's phrase in "What Then Is the American, This New Man?" *American Historical Review*, XLVIII (January, 1943), 241.

9. Arrington, *op. cit.*, p. 51.

10. Edward Smith, *Account of a Journey Through North-Eastern Texas* (London, 1849), p. 7.

11. *Western Monthly Magazine*, II (October, 1834), 660.

12. *Spirit of the Times*, March 7, 1840.

13. *Galveston Texas Times*, December 7, 1842.

14. *Telegraph and Texas Register*, March 27, 1839.

15. *Victoria Texian Advocate*, Jan. 12, 1849.

16. Haldeen Braddy, "Tall Talk of the Texas Trans Pecos," *American Speech*, XV (1940), 220-22.

17. Quoted in Mody C. Boatright, "More About 'Hell in Texas,'" in *From Hell to Breakfast*, pp. 135-36.

18. This appeared in print most recently in Stanley Walker's "Everything's True About Texas," *Harper's Magazine*, CC (March, 1950), 36.

19. Walter Blair has suggested this as a prime factor in the presence of exaggeration in all western humor.

20. *Spirit of the Times*, December 11, 1847.

21. *Texas and the Gulf of Mexico; or Yachting in the New World* (London, 1844), II, 107.

22. *The American Joe Miller* (1840), p. 155.

23. *Philadelphia Sunday Dispatch*, July 20, 1862.

24. *Flag of Our Union*, December 11, 1847.

25. *Texas Gazette*, March 27, 1830.

26. Donald Day, "Leaves of Mesquite Grass," in *From Hell to Breakfast*, p. 67, quoting an early Texas newspaper.

27. *Ibid.*, p. 67.

28. *Ibid.*, p. 70.

29. *Col. Crockett's Exploits and Adventures in Texas*, p. 86. Under the title, "A Texan," this passage appears in the *Spirit of the Times*, October 1, 1836.

30. Mrs. Holley, *Texas*, p. 118.

Chapter Seven

1. T. C. Haliburton, *The Clockmaker; or, the Sayings and Doings of Sam Slick of Slickville* (New York, 1843), p. 39.

2. A. A. Parker, *Trip to the West and Texas* (Concord, New Hampshire, 1835), p. 174.

3. *Spirit of the Times*, June 10, 1837.

4. Richard M. Dorson gives this as a possible explanation of much of the uncouthness in western humor. See his *Davy Crockett: American Comic Legend* (New York, 1939), p. xx.

5. Hooton, *op. cit.*, p. 15.

6. *Ibid.*, p. 16.

7. *Ibid.*, p. 35.

8. *Ibid.*, p. 116.

9. *Ibid.*, p. 72.

10. *Ibid.*, p. 117.

11. T. A. Morris, *Miscellany: Consisting of Essays, Biographical Sketches, and Notes of Travel* (Cincinnati, 1852), p. 318.

12. Olmsted, *op. cit.*, p. 75.

13. *Ibid.*, p. 121.

14. Frederick Marryat, *The Travels and Adventures of Monsieur Violet in California, Sonora, and Western Texas* (1843), p. 346.

15. W. L. Courtney in his Introduction to the Boston, 1898 edition of *The Travels*.

16. Marryat, *op. cit.*, p. 143.

17. *Ibid.*, p. 141.

18. *Ibid.*, p. 145.

19. *Loc. cit.*

20. *Ibid.*, p. 208.

21. *Spirit of the Times*, March 23, 1844.

22. Mrs. Viele, *op. cit.*, pp. 96-97.

23. *Ibid.*, p. 107.

24. F. B. Page, *Prairiedom: Rambles and Scrambles in Texas or New Estremadura* (New York, 1845), p. 14.

25. P. 64 in the book form of his articles, *Texas: Sketches of Character; Moral and Political Condition of the Republic; the Judiciary &c* (Philadelphia, 1839).

26. [Anonymous], *A Visit to Texas* (New York, 2nd ed., 1836), p. 118.

27. Matilda Houstoun, *Texas and the Gulf of Mexico; or Yachting in the New World* (London, 1844), II, 98.

28. *Ibid.*, II, 102.

29. Matilda Houstoun, *Hesperos: or, Travels in the West* (London, 1850), II, 139.

30. J. O. Andrew, *Miscellanies: Comprising Letters, Essays and Addresses* (Louisville, Kentucky, 1854), p. 115.

31. George Bonnell, *Topographical Description of Texas* (Austin, Texas, 1840), p. 118.

32. Morris, *op. cit.*, p. 324.

33. Page, *op. cit.*, p. 20.

34. *Houston Telegraph and Texas Register*, December 19, 1838.

35. *Niles Register*, April 19, 1834.

36. *Houston National Intelligencer*, March 28, 1839.

37. Philip Ashton Rollins, *The Cowboy* (New York, 1924), p. 72.

38. Parker, *op. cit.*, p. 178.

39. Mrs. Viele, *op. cit.*, p. 150.

40. *Ibid.*, p. 81.

41. *Ibid.*, p. 107.

42. Cora Montgomery, *Eagle Pass; or Life on the Border* (New York, 1852), p. 16.

43. Mrs. Viele, *op. cit.*, p. 148.

44. William Kennedy, *Texas: Its Geography, Natural History, and Topography* (New York edition, 1844), p. 47.

Chapter Eight

1. *Pennsylvanian*, August 15, 1853.

2. The references to the drama here are all taken from the novel form.

3. Quoted in Arthur Hobson Quinn, *History of the American Drama from the Beginning to the Civil War* (New York, 1923), p. 294.

4. *Ibid.*, p. 278.

5. *Picayune,* November 18, 1838.

6. Joseph N. Ireland, *Records of the New York Stage* (New York, 1867), II, 431.

7. *London Theatrical Observer,* Mar. 14, 1844.

8. "The Philadelphia Stage," *Philadelphia Sunday Dispatch,* February 9, 1862.

9. Emerson Bennett, *Clara Moreland; or, Adventures in the Far Southwest* (Philadelphia, 1853), p. 300.

10. During the years of the Mexican War appeared several other plays about it which probably included Texans, though without the actual texts it is impossible to say definitely. Their titles were: *Siege of Monterrey,* which played in Philadelphia, October, 1846, and in New York, September, 1847; a different *Campaign on the Rio Grande,* in New York, July, 1846: *Le Capitaine May et Le General de la Vega sur le Bords du Rio Grande,* in New Orleans, May, 1847; *Cerro Gordo,* in Philadelphia, June, 1847; *Our Flag Is Nailed to the Mast,* in Philadelphia, July, 1845; *Victory Upon Victory; Seeing the Elephant,* in Philadelphia, January, 1848, and in New York, September, 1848; and *The Battle of Mexico,* in New York, January, 1848.

11. Ireland, *Records of the New York Stage,* II, 480.

12. Number 100 in DeWitt's "Acting Plays" (New York, about 1850).

13. Charles Wilkins Webber, *Jack Long: or Shot in the Eye* (New York, 1846), p. 1.

14. *Portland Daily American,* November 5, 1844.

15. This play was printed in the *Southern Literary Messenger,* XVIII (1852), and appeared the same year in pamphlet form from the same publisher.

16. *Charleston Courier,* March 26, 1855.

17. William P. Trent, *William Gilmore Simms* (New York, 1892), p. 216.

Chapter Nine

1. *The Devil's Comical Texas Oldmanick: with Comic Engravings of all the Principal Events of Texas* (Philadelphia and New York, 1836), p. 11.

2. *Rough and Ready Almanac for 1849* (Philadelphia), no page.

3. *Ibid.,* no page.

4. *The Devil's Comical Texas Oldmanick,* no page.

5. Fisher's Comic Almanac (1841), p. 21.

6. *The Old American Comic Almanac* (Boston, 1843), p. 28.

7. According to Crockett's biographer, James A. Shackford.

8. See his Introduction to Richard M. Dorson's *Davy Crockett: American Comic Legend* (New York, 1939), and also Constance Rourke's *Davy Crockett* (New York, 1934), p. 249.

9. Rourke, *op. cit.,* p. 247.

10. *Davy Crockett's Almanack, of Wild Sports in the West, Life in the Backwoods, and Sketches of Texas,* pp. 2-3.

11. *The Squatter's Almanac* (New York and Philadelphia, 1845), no page.

12. *Crockett's Almanac, Containing Life, Manners and Adventures in the Back Woods, and Rows, Sprees, and Scrapes on the Western Waters* (Philadelphia, New York, and Boston, 1851), no page.

13. *Davy Crockett's Almanac; Daring Adventures in the Back Woods; Wonderful Scenes in River Life; Manners of Warfare in the West; Feats on the Prairies, in Texas and Oregon* (New York, 1847), no page.

14. *Crockett's Almanac; Scenes in River Life, Feats on the Lakes, Manners in the Backwoods, Adventures in Texas &c &c* (Philadelphia and Boston, 1846), no page.

15. *Crockett Almanac, Containing Life, Manners, and Adventures in the Backwoods, and Rows, Sprees, and Scrapes on the Western Waters* (New York, 1854), no page.

16. *Crockett's Almanac* (Philadelphia and Boston, 1846), p. 18.

17. *Crockett's Almanac* (Philadelphia, New York, and Boston, 1851), no page.

18. Quoted in the *New York Spirit of the Times*, July 11, 1846.

19. *Crockett's Almanac* (Boston, 1848), no page.

20. *The Devil's Comical Texas Oldmanick*, p. 4.

21. *Ben Hardin's Crockett Almanac, Rows, Sprees, and Scrapes in the West; Life and Manners in the Backwoods; and Terrible Adventures on the Ocean* (Baltimore, 1842), p. 9.

22. *Crockett's Almanac* (Boston, 1848), no page.

23. *Ben Hardin's Crockett Almanac* (Baltimore, 1842), p. 17.

24. *The Squatter's Almanac* (New York and Philadelphia, 1845), no page.

25. *Davy Crockett's Almanac* (New York, 1847), no page.

26. *Ibid.*, no page.

Chapter Ten

1. Mrs. Viele, *op. cit.*, p. 146.

2. Noah Webster to Mathew Carey, August 14, 1791, quoted in Earl L. Bradsher, *Mathew Carey, Editor, Author, and Publisher* (New York, 1912), p. 128.

3. Bradsher, *op. cit.*, p. 85.

4. Bradsher, "Book Publishers and Book Publishing," *The Cambridge History of American Literature* (New York, 1921), IV, 549.

5. Judson to William Henry Venable, April 10, 1885, quoted in Venable's *Beginning of Literary Culture in the Ohio Valley* (Cincinnati, 1891), p. 295.

6. *Time Magazine*, LVI (July 10, 1950), 82.

7. Article on Judson, *Appleton's Cyclopaedia of American Biography* (New York, 1915), no page.

8. Luke White, Jr., *Henry William Herbert and the American Publishing Scene* (Newark, New Jersey, 1943), p. 4.

9. *Ibid.*, p. 27.

10. Charles Wilkins Webber, *The Prairie Scout* (New York, 1852), p. 6.

11. James Wilmer Dallam, *The Lone Star; a Tale of Texas; Founded Upon Incidents in the History of Texas* (New York, 1845), p. 20.

12. *Ibid.*, p. 6.

13. *Ibid.*, preface.

14. *Knickerbocker*, XXIV (December, 1844), 583.

15. Quoted in James A. Harrison, *The Complete Works of Edgar Allan Poe* (New York, 1902), XV, 188.

16. Longfellow's diary entry for March 6, 1846, quoted in Samuel Longfellow, *Life of Henry Wadsworth Longfellow with Extracts from His Journals and Correspondence* (Boston, 1886), II, 35.

17. Joseph Holt Ingraham, *The Texan Ranger; or, the Maid of Matamoras, a Tale of the Mexican War* (c1847), p. 85.

18. Evart A. and George L. Duyckinck, *Cyclopaedia of American Literature* (New York, 1855), II, 667.

19. But profited from it too, when he copied seventy pages verbatim from Charles Sealsfield's Bob Rock story in *The Cabin Book* into his *The Prairie Scout*.

20. Charles Wilkins Webber, *Tales of the Southern Border*, p. 9.

21. *Ibid.*, p. 13.

22. Webber, *Jack Long; or Shot in the Eye* (New York, 1846), p. 4.

23. Newton Mallory Curtis, *The Hunted Chief: or, the Female Ranchero* (1847), p. 5.

24. E. Z. C. Judson, *The Volunteer: or, the Maid of Monterey* (1847), p. 16.

25. Charles E. Averill, *Mexican Ranchero: or, the Maid of the Chapparal* (1847), p. 63.

26. James Wilmer Dallam, *The Deaf Spy* (Baltimore, 1848), p. 23.

27. Hunt, *Frank Forester [Henry William Herbert] a Tragedy in Exile* (Newark, New Jersey, 1933), p. 106.

28. Henry William Herbert, *Pierre, the Partisan: a Tale of the Mexican Marches* (1848), p. 6.

29. *Ibid.*, p. 65.

30. *Godey's Lady's Book,* quoted in E. Douglas Branch's *The Sentimental Years 1836-1860* (New York, 1934), p. 128.
31. C. Chauncey Burr, *An Essay on the Writings and Genius of George Lippard* (Philadelphia, 1847), p. XXVI.
32. George Lippard, *'Bel of Prairie Eden: a Romance of Mexico* (1848), p. 16.
33. John Hovey Robinson, *The Lone Star: or, the Texan Bravo* (1852), p. 15.

Chapter Eleven

1. *Literary World,* II (Oct., 1848), 310.
2. George Lippard, *Legends of Mexico* (1847), p. 14.
3. *Ibid.,* p. 19.
4. Arrington, *op. cit.,* p. 50.
5. *Ibid.,* p. 62.
6. John Tomlin, *Tales of the Caddo* (1849), p. 44.
7. *Norton's Literary Gazette* (July 15, 1853), p. 118.
8. *Southern Quarterly Review,* VIII (July, 1852), 251.
9. Webber, *Tales of the Southern Border,* p. 79.
10. *Ibid.,* p. 54.
11. Emerson Bennett, *Forest and Prairie: or, Life on the Frontier* (1860), p. 371.
12. *Loc. cit.*
13. He copied the Punch and Judy show scene in Little Rock from A. B. Longstreet's *Georgia Scenes.*
14. "Biography of Richard Penn Smith," *Burton's Gentleman's Magazine,* V (September, 1839), 121.
15. [Richard Penn Smith], *Col. Crockett's Exploits and Adventures in Texas* (1836), p. 131.
16. *Western Monthly Magazine,* V (October, 1836), 625.
17. Timothy Flint's *Francis Berrian, or the Mexican Patriot* (Boston, 1826), is laid in Texas during Mexico's struggle for independence from Spain. Its period is much too early to allow for a description of Texas Anglo-American settlement.
18. Anthony Ganilh, *Mexico Versus Texas* (1838), p. 199.
19. *Ibid.,* p. 263.

20. "Charles Sealsfield" was the pseudonym of Karl Anton Postl. Quoted in Otto Heller and Theodore H. Leon, *Charles Sealsfield,* Washington University Studies—New Series, Language and Literature—Number 8 (St. Louis, September, 1939), p. 80.
21. *Knickerbocker Magazine,* XXIV (August, 1844), 185.
22. Quoted in Bernhard A. Uhlendorf, *Charles Sealsfield: Ethnic Elements and National Problems in His Works,* p. 17.
23. Charles Sealsfield, *The Cabin Book, or Sketches of Life in Texas,* p. 9.
24. *Ibid.,* p. 10.
25. *Spirit of the Times,* April 22, 1848.
26. *Graham's,* XXXII (June, 1848), 356.
27. *Old Hicks the Guide,* in the *New York Sunday Dispatch,* July 25, 1847, no page.
28. *Ibid.,* June 27, 1847.
29. Charles Wilkins Webber, *The Prairie Scout, or Agatone the Renegade* (1852), p. 40.
30. *Ibid.,* p. 40.
31. *Ibid.,* p. 165.
32. *Ibid.,* p. 246.
33. Webber, *The Gold Mines of the Gila* (1849), p. 193.
34. Samuel Hammett, *A Stray Yankee in Texas* (1853), p. XIV.
35. *Ibid.,* p. 351.
36. *Ibid.,* p. 325.
37. Jeremiah Clemens, *Bernard Lile; an Historical Romance* (1856), p. 101.
38. *Ibid.,* p. 110.
39. *Russell's,* II (December, 1857), 285.
40. J. Frank Dobie, "Mustang Gray: Fact, Tradition, and Song," *Tone the Bell Easy,* "Publications of the Texas Folk-lore Society," X (Austin, Texas, 1932), 112.
41. Alfred W. Arrington, *The Rangers and Regulators of the Tanaha: or, Life Among the Lawless* (1856), p. 145.
42. *Ibid.,* p. 208.

Chapter Twelve

1. T. J. Wertenbaker, *The Old South* (New York, 1942), p. 18.

BIBLIOGRAPHY

The books behind this book are many, but their number does not necessarily make them easy to find. Most are now obtainable only in the rare book collections in this country's largest libraries. Below are listed the full titles of all the primary materials which I found valuable. The libraries where they are available are indicated by the symbols: LC—Library of Congress, NYPL—New York Public Library, Y—Yale University Library, AAS—American Antiquarian Society in Worcester, Massachusetts, UT—University of Texas Library, H—Harvard University Library, UV—University of Virginia Library. Secondary works particularly relevant to my study are few; the items whose titles appear below in this group are only those which were of a very special value in the clarification of certain aspects of my subject. I shall make no attempt to include here the titles of all other secondary sources which I used, or those which I may have cited in footnotes; most of these are general treatments of the Westward Movement and are so well known as to make the inclusion of their titles here seem unnecessary.

BOOKS (primary)

American Joe Miller, The. Philadelphia, 1840. (LC)

ANDREW, J. O. *Miscellanies: Comprising Letters, Essays, and Addresses; to Which Is Added a Biographical Sketch of Mrs. Ann Amelia Andrew.* Louisville, 1854. (UT)

[ARRINGTON, ALFRED W.] *Desperadoes of the Southwest, Containing an Account of the Canehill Murders, Together with the Lives of Several of the Most Notorious Regulators and Moderators of that Region.* New York, 1847. (LC)

———. *The Lives and Adventures of the Desperadoes of the Southwest, Containing an Account of the Duelists and Dueling Together with the Lives of Several of the Most Notorious Regulators and Moderators of that Region.* New York, 1849. (LC)

———. *Poems, by Alfred W. Arrington with a Sketch of his Character and a Memoir.* Chicago, 1869. (LC)

———. *The Rangers and Regulators of the Tanaha: or, Life Among the Lawless, a Tale of the Republic of Texas.* New York, 1856. (LC)

AVERILL, CHARLES E. *Mexican Ranchero: or, the Maid of the Chapparal.* Boston, 1847. (UT)

BALDWIN, JOSEPH G[LOVER]. *The Flush Times of Alabama and Mississippi, a Series of Sketches.* New York, 1853. (LC)

BARTLETT, JOHN RUSSELL. *Personal Narrative of Explorations and Incidents in Texas, New Mexico, California, Sonora, and Chihuahua.* London, New York, 1854. (UT)

BENNETT, EMERSON. *Clara Moreland; or, Adventures in the Far South-west. Embellished with Magnificent Illustrations.* Philadelphia, 1853. (LC)

———. *Forest and Prairie; or, Life on the Frontier.* Philadelphia, 1860. (LC)

———. *Viola; or, Adventures in the Far Southwest.* Philadelphia [1854]. (LC)

BONNELL, GEORGE W. *Topographical Description of Texas, to Which Is Added an Account of the Indian Tribes.* Austin, Texas, 1840. (UT)

BRINLEY, FRANCIS. *Life of William T. Porter.* New York, 1860. (LC)

BURR, C. CHAUNCEY. *An Essay on the Writings and Genius of George Lippard.* Philadelphia, 1847. (LC)

CAREY, HENRY CHARLES. *Letters on International Copyright.* Philadelphia, 1853. (LC)

[CARRUTHERS, WILLIAM ALEXANDER]. *The Kentuckian in New York; or, the Adventures of Three Southerns.* New York, 1834. (UT)

CHANNING, WILLIAM E. *A Letter to the Hon. Henry Clay, on the Annexation of Texas to the United States.* Boston, 1837. (UT)

CHILD, DAVID LEE. *The Texan Revolution, Republished with Additions from the Northampton (Massachusetts) Gazette, to Which Is Added a Letter from Washington on the Annexation of Texas, and the Late Outrage in California.* n. p., n. d. (UT)

CLAPP, WILLIAM W., JR. *A Record of the Boston Stage.* Boston, 1853. (LC)

CLEMENS, JEREMIAH. *Bernard Lile; an Historical Romance, Embracing the Periods of the Texas Revolution and the Mexican War.* Philadelphia, 1856. (LC)

——. *Mustang Gray; a Romance.* Philadelphia, 1858. (LC)

[CLEVELAND, ALICE]. *Lucy Morley: or, the Young Officer, a Tale of the Texan Revolution.* Boston, 1846. (H)

CLODPOLE, CHRISTOPHER. *The Clodpole Papers, Containing the Incidents, Adventures, Wise Sayings, Shrewd Remarks, Philosophical Disquisitions, Political Opinions, and Theological Lectures, of Christopher Clodpole, Esq. Farmer.* Baltimore, 1844. (LC)

[COLTON, REV. CALEB]. *Annexation of Texas, by Junius.* The Junius Tracts, No. IX. New York, 1844. (LC)

COWELL, JOE. *Thirty Years Passed Among the Players in England and America: Interspersed with Anecdotes and Reminiscences of a Variety of Persons, Directly or Indirectly Connected with the Drama During the Theatrical Life of Joe Cowell, Comedian.* New York, 1844. (LC)

CROCKETT, DAVID. *An Account of Col. Crockett's Tour to the North and Down East, in the Year of Our Lord One Thousand Eight Hundred and Thirty-four.* Philadelphia, 1835. (UT)

——. *Narrative of the Life of David Crockett of West Tennessee.* Philadelphia, Baltimore and London, 1834. (LC)

——. *Sketches and Eccentricities of Col. David Crockett, of West Tennessee.* New York, 1833. (LC)

CURTIS, NEWTON M. *The Prairie Guide: or, the Rose of the Rio Grande.* New York [c1847]. (Y)

——. *The Hunted Chief; or, The Female Ranchero, a Tale of the Mexican War.* New York, 1847. (LC)

CUSHING, S. W. *Wild Oats Sowings; or the Autobiography of an Adventurer.* New York, 1857. (UT)

[DALLAM, JAMES W.] *The Deaf Spy, A Tale Founded Upon Incidents in the History of Texas, by the Author of the "Lone Star."* Baltimore, 1848. (LC)

DALLAM, JAMES W. *The Lone Star: a Tale of Texas; Founded Upon Incidents in the History of Texas.* New York, 1845. (UT)

DAVIDGE, WILLIAM. *Footlight Flashes.* New York, 1866. (LC)

DEWEES, W. B. *Letters from an Early Settler of Texas, Compiled by Cara Cardelle.* Louisville, Kentucky, 1852. (UT)

DEWEY, ORVILLE. *On American Morals and Manners*. Boston, 1844. (LC)

DOMENECH, ABBE. *Missionary Adventures in Texas and Mexico, A Personal Narrative of Six Years' Sojourn in those Regions*. Translated from the French. London, 1858. (UT)

DUVAL, JOHN C. *The Adventures of Big-foot Wallace, the Texas Ranger and Hunter*. [Macon, Georgia], 1870. (UT)

DWIGHT, TIMOTHY. *Travels in New England and New York*. 4 vols. New Haven, Connecticut, 1821-22. (LC)

EDWARD, DAVID B. *The History of Texas; or, the Emigrant's, Farmer's, and Politician's Guide to the Character, Climate, Soil and Productions of the Country; Geographically Arranged from Personal Observation and Experience*. Cincinnati, 1836. (UT)

ENGLISH, THOMAS DUNN. *1844; or, The Power of "S. F.," a Tale; Developing the Secret Action of Parties During the Presidential Campaign of 1844*. New York, 1847. (LC)

FEATHERSTONHAUGH, G. W. *Excursion Through the Slave States, from Washington on the Potomac to the Frontier of Mexico, with Sketches of Popular Manners and Geological Notices*. 2 vols. London, 1844. (UT)

FERRALL, S. A. *A Ramble of Six Thousand Miles Through the United States of America*. London, 1832. (UT)

FISHER, ORCENETH. *Sketches of Texas in 1840; Designed to Answer in a Brief Way, the Numerous Enquiries Respecting the New Republic, as to Situation, Extent, Climate, Soil, Productions, Water, Government, Society, Religion, etc.* Springfield, Illinois, 1841. (UT)

[FISKE?]. *A Visit to Texas; Being the Journal of a Traveller Through Those Parts Most Interesting to American Settlers, With Descriptions of Scenery, Habits, etc.* 2nd ed. New York, 1836. (Y)

FLAGG, WILSON. *The Tailor's Shop; or, Crowns of Thorns and Coats of Thistles, Designed to Tickle Some and Nettle Others; Intended Chiefly for Politicians, Inscribed to Those Whom They May Fit*. Boston, 1844. (LC)

FLINT, TIMOTHY. *Francis Berrian: or, The Mexican Patriot*. Boston, 1826. (LC)

[FLINT, TIMOTHY]. *George Mason, the Young Backwoodsman; or Don't Give up the Ship, a Story of the Mississippi*. Boston, 1829. (LC)

————. *Recollections of the Last Ten Years, Passed in Occasional Residences and Journeyings in the Valley of the Mississippi, From Pittsburgh and the Missouri to the Gulf of Mexico, and From Florida to the Spanish Frontier; in a Series of Letters to the Rev. James Flint, of Salem, Massachusetts*. Boston, 1826. (LC)

FOLSON, CHARLES J. *Mexico in 1842: a Description of the Country, Its Natural and Political Features; with a Sketch of Its History, Brought Down to the Present Year, to Which Is Added an Account of Texas and Yucatan*. New York, 1842. (UT)

FOOTE, HENRY STUART. *Texas and the Texans; or, Advance of the Anglo-Americans to the South-west; Including a History of Leading Events in Mexico, from the Conquest by Fernando Cortes to the Termination of the Texan Revolution*. Philadelphia, 1841. (Y)

FORREST, COL. CRIS. *Jack Long; or, the Shot in the Eye, a Tale of Cruel Wrong and Wild Revenge.* New York, 1868. (LC)

FROEBEL, JULIUS. *Seven Years' Travel in Central America, Northern Mexico, and the Far West of the United States.* London, 1859. (UT)

FROST, J[OHN]. *The Mexican War and Its Warriors; Comprising a Complete History of All the Operations of the American Armies in Mexico; With Biographical Sketches and Anecdotes of the Most Distinguished Officers in the Regular Army and Volunteer Force.* New Haven and Philadelphia, 1850. (UT)

FROST, JOHN. *Thrilling Adventures Among the Indians: Comprising the Most Remarkable Personal Narratives of Events in the Early Indian Wars, As Well As of Incidents in the Recent Indian Hostilities in Mexico and Texas.* Philadelphia, 1857. (UT)

[GANILH, ANTHONY?] *Mexico Versus Texas, a Descriptive Novel.* Philadelphia, 1838. (LC)

General Taylor and His Staff: Comprising Memoirs of Generals Taylor, Worth, Wool, and Butler: Colonels May, Cross, Clay, Hardin, Yell, Hays, and Other Distinguished Officers Attached to General Taylor's Army; Interspersed with Numerous Anecdotes of the Mexican War, and Personal Adventures of the Officers, Compiled from Public Documents and Private Correspondence. Philadelphia, 1848. (LC)

General Taylor and the Mexican War. n. p. [1847?]. (UT)

GREELEY, HORACE. *Recollections of a Busy Life: Including Reminiscences of American Politics and Politicians, from the Opening of the Missouri Contest to the Downfall of Slavery; to Which Are Added Miscellanies: "Literature as a Vocation," "Poets and Poetry," "Reforms and Reformers," A Defence of Protection, etc., Also, A Discussion with Robert Dale Owen of the Law of Divorce.* New York, 1868. (LC)

GREGG, JOSIAH. *Commerce of the Prairies or the Journal of a Santa Fe Trader, During Eight Expeditions Across the Great Western Prairies, and a Residence of Nearly Nine Years in Northern Mexico.* New York, 1844. (LC)

GRISWOLD, RUFUS WILMOT. *The Prose Writers of America: With a Survey of the Intellectual History, Condition, and Prospects of the Country.* 3rd ed. Philadelphia, 1849. (LC)

HALE, EDWARD EVERETT. *G. T. T. ; or, the Wonderful Adventures of a Pullman.* Boston, 1877. (LC)

[HALIBURTON, THOMAS CHANDLER]. *The Americans at Home; or, Byeways, Backwoods, and Prairies.* 3 vols. London, 1854. (LC)

————. *The Clockmaker; or, the Sayings and Doings of Sam Slick of Slickville.* 2nd ser. New York, 1843. (UT)

————. *Nature and Human Nature.* New York, 1855. (UT)

HALYARD, HARRY. *The Heroine of Tampico; or, Wildfire the Wanderer, a Tale of the Mexican War.* Boston, 1848. (LC)

————. *The Mexican Spy: or, the Bride of Buena Vista, a Tale of the Mexican War.* Boston, 1848. (LC)

————. *The Ocean Monarch; or, the Ranger of the Gulf, a Mexican Romance.* Boston, 1848. (LC)

HAMMETT, SAMUEL A. *Piney Woods Tavern: or, Sam Slick in Texas.* Philadelphia, 1858. (LC)

[HAMMETT, SAMUEL ADAMS]. *A Stray Yankee in Texas.* New York, 1853. (H)

HENRY, CAPTAIN W. S. *Campaign Sketches of the War with Mexico.* New York, 1847. (LC)

HERBERT, HENRY WILLIAM. *Pierre, the Partisan; a Tale of the Mexican Marches.* New York, 1848. (LC)

HOLLEY, MARY AUSTIN. *Texas; Observations, Historical, Geographical and Descriptive in a Series of Letters.* Baltimore, 1833. (LC)

HONE, PHILIP. *The Diary of Philip Hone, 1828-1851.* Ed. with Intro. by Allan Nevins. 2 vols. New York, 1927. (LC)

HOOTON, CHARLES. *St. Louis' Isle, or Texiana; with Additional Observations Made in the United States and in Canada.* London, 1847. (UT)

HOUSTON, SAM. *Speeches of Sam Houston, of Texas, in Reference to the Military Occupation of Santa Fe, and in Defence of Texas and the Texian Volunteers in the Mexican War.* n. p., 1850. (UT)

HOUSTOUN, MRS. [MATILDA CHARLOTTE]. *Hesperos: or, Travels in the West.* London, 1850. (UT)

———. *Texas and the Gulf of Mexico; or Yachting in the New World.* London, 1844. (UT)

IKIN, ARTHUR. *Texas: Its History, Topography, Agriculture, Commerce, and General Statistics.* London, 1841. (UT)

[INGRAHAM, JOSEPH HOLT]. *Lafitte: the Pirate of the Gulf, by the Author of "The Southwest."* 2 vols. New York, 1836. (LC)

INGRAHAM, J[OSEPH] H[OLT]. *The Texan Ranger: or, The Maid of Matamoras, a Tale of the Mexican War.* 2nd ed. New York [c1847] (pp. 64-112 of Curtis, *The Prairie Guide).* (Y) The first edition appeared in Boston, 1846.

IRELAND, JOSEPH N. *Records of the New York Stage, from 1750 to 1860.* New York, 1867. (LC)

IRVING, WASHINGTON. *Knickerbocker's History of New York,* Kaaterskill Edition. New York, 1879. (LC)

[JUDSON, EDWARD Z. C.]. *The Volunteer; or, the Maid of Monterey, A Tale of the Mexican War.* Boston, 1847. (Y)

KENDALL, GEORGE WILKINS. *Narrative of the Texan Santa Fe Expedition, Comprising a Description of a Tour Through Texas, and Across the Great Southwestern Prairies, the Camanche [sic] and Caygua Hunting Grounds, With an Account of the Sufferings from Want of Food, Losses from Hostile Indians, and Final Capture of the Texans, and Their March, as Prisoners, to the City of Mexico.* 2 vols. London, 1844. (UT)

———. *The War Between the United States and Mexico Illustrated, Embracing Pictorial Drawings of all the Principal Conflicts, by Carl Nebel, with a Description of Each Battle, by Geo. Wilkins Kendall.* New York, 1851. (UT)

KENNEDY, WILLIAM. *Texas; Its Geography, Natural History, and Topography.* New York, 1844. (Y)

KERR, HUGH. *A Poetical Description of Texas, and Narrative of Many Interesting Events in that Country, Embracing a Period of Several Years, Interspersed with Moral and Political Impressions: Also, an Appeal to Those Who Oppose the Union of Texas with the United States, and the Anticipation of that Event, to Which Is Added, The Texas Heroes.* New York, 1838. (LC)

[LAWRENCE, A. B.?]. *Texas in 1840, or the Emigrant's Guide to the New Republic; Being the Result of Observation, Enquiry and Travel in that Beautiful Country.* New York, 1840. (UT)

LEE, NELSON. *Three Years Among the Camanches [sic], the Narrative of Nelson Lee, the Texan Ranger, Containing a Detailed Account of His Captivity Among the Indians, His Singular Escape Through the Instrumentality of His Watch, and Fully Illustrating Indian Life as It Is on the War Path and in the Camp.* Albany, New York, 1859. (UT)

LEMAN, WALTER M. *Memories of an Old Actor.* San Francisco, 1886. (LC)

LESTER, C. EDWARDS. *Sam Houston and His Republic.* New York, 1846. (UT)

[LEWIS, HENRY C.]. *Odd Leaves from the Life of a Louisiana "Swamp Doctor."* Philadelphia, 1843. (LC)

LIPPARD, GEORGE. *'Bel of Prairie Eden, a Romance of Mexico.* Boston, 1848. (LC)

——. *Legends of Mexico.* Philadelphia, 1847. (LC)

LUDLOW, N[OAH] M[ILLER]. *Dramatic Life As I Found It; a Record of Personal Experience; with an Account of the Rise and Progress of the Drama in the West and South, with Anecdotes and Biographical Sketches of the Principal Actors and Actresses Who Have at Times Appeared upon the Stage in the Mississippi Valley.* St. Louis, 1880. (UV)

LUFF, LORRY. *Antonita, The Female Contrabandista, a Mexican Tale of Land and Water.* New York, 1848. (LC)

——. *The Texan Captain and the Female Smuggler, a Mexican Tale of Land and Water.* New York, 1850. (LC)

LUNDY, BENJAMIN. *The Life, Travels and Opinions of Benjamin Lundy, Including His Journeys to Texas and Mexico, With a Sketch of Cotemporary [sic] Events, and a Notice of the Revolution in Hayti, Compiled under the Direction and on Behalf of His Children.* Philadelphia, 1847. (UT)

LYELL, SIR CHARLES. *A Second Visit to the United States of North America.* London, 1850. (UT)

McCALLA, W. L. *Adventures in Texas, Chiefly in the Spring and Summer of 1840; with a Discussion of Comparative Character, Political, Religious, and Moral.* Philadelphia, 1841. (UT)

McCONNEL, J. L. *Western Characters, or Types of Border Life in the Western States.* New York, 1853. (UT)

MAILLARD, N. DORAN. *The History of the Republic of Texas, Discovery of the Country to the Present Time; and the Cause of Her Separation from the Republic of Mexico.* London, 1842. (UT)

MARRYAT, FLORENCE. *Life and Letters of Captain Marryat.* New York, 1872. (LC)

MARRYAT, CAPTAIN FREDERICK. *Percival Keene.* New York, 1842. (LC)

——. *The Travels and Adventures of Monsieur Violet in California, Sonora, and Western Texas.* London, 1843. (LC)

MELISH, JOHN. *Travels in the United States of America in the Years 1806 and 1807, and 1809, 1810, and 1811; Including an Account of Passages Betwixt America and Britain, and Travels Through Various Parts of Great Britain, Ireland, and Upper Canada.* Philadelphia, 1812. (UT)

MIDDLETON, JONH [sic] H. *History of the Regulators and Moderators and Shelby County War in 1841 and 1842, in the Republic of Texas, with Facts and Incidents in the Early History of the Republic and State, from 1837 to the Annexation, Together with Incidents of Frontier Life and Indian Troubles, and the War on the Reserve in Young County in 1857.* Fort Worth, Texas, 1883. (LC)

MONTGOMERY, CORA. *Eagle Pass; or, Life on the Border.* New York, 1852. (UT)

MOORE, FRANCIS, JR. *Map and Description of Texas, Containing Sketches of Its History, Geology, Geography and Statistics; With Concise Statements, Relative to the Soil, Climate, Productions, Facilities of Transportation, Population of the Country; and Some Brief Remarks Upon the Character and Customs of Its Inhabitants.* Philadelphia, 1840. (UT)

MORRIS, T. A. *Miscellany: Consisting of Essays, Biographical Sketches, and Notes of Travel.* Cincinnati, 1852. (UT)

MURAT, ACHILLE. *America and the Americans.* Buffalo, New York, 1849. (UT)

NEWELL, CHESTER. *History of the Revolution in Texas, Particularly of the War of 1835 and '36; Together with the Latest Geographical, Topographical, and Statistical Accounts of the Country, from the Most Authentic Sources.* New York, 1838. (UT)

Notions of the Americans: Picked up by a Travelling Bachelor. 2 vols. Philadelphia, 1828. (UT)

OLMSTED, FREDERICK LAW. *A Journey Through Texas: Or, a Saddle-trip on the Southwestern Frontier: with a Statistical Appendix.* New York, 1857. (UT)

[PAGE, DR. F. B.]. *Prairiedom: Rambles and Scrambles in Texas or New Estremadura.* New York, 1845. (UT)

PARKER, A. A. *Trip to the West and Texas, Comprising a Journey of Eight Thousand Miles, Through New-York, Michigan, Illinois, Missouri, Louisiana, and Texas, in the Autumn and Winter of 1834-5, Interspersed with Anecdotes, Incidents and Observations.* Concord, New Hampshire, 1835. (UT)

PATTIE, JAMES O. *The Personal Narrative of James O. Pattie, of Kentucky, during an Expedition from St. Louis, Through the Vast Regions Between that Place and the Pacific Ocean, and Thence Back Through the City of Mexico to Vera Cruz, during Journeyings of Six Years: in Which He and His Father, Who Accompanied Him, Suffered Unheard of Hardships and Dangers, Had Various Conflicts with the Indians, and Were Made Captives, in Which Captivity His Father Died; Together with a Description of the Country, and the Various Nations Through Which They Passed.* Edited by Timothy Flint. Cincinnati, 1833. (LC)

PECK, JOHN MASON. *A New Guide for Emigrants to the West, Containing Sketches of Michigan, Ohio, Indiana, Illinois, Missouri, Arkansas, with the Territory of Wisconsin and the Adjacent Parts.* Boston, 1837. (LC)

PORTER, WILLIAM T. *The Big Bear of Arkansas, and Other Sketches, Illustrative of Characters and Incidents in the South and South-west.* Philadelphia, 1845. (LC)

———. *Colonel Thorpe's Scenes in Arkansaw.* Philadelphia, 1858. (LC)

———. *A Quarter Race in Kentucky, and Other Sketches, Illustrative of Scenes, Characters, and Incidents, Throughout the "Universal Yankee Nation."* Philadelphia, 1847. (LC)

[PRAY, ISAAC C.]. *Memoirs of James Gordon Bennett and His Times.* New York, 1855. (LC)

RANKIN, MELINDA. *Texas in 1850.* Boston, 1850. (UT)

REES, JAMES. *The Dramatic Authors of America.* Philadelphia, 1845. (LC)

REID, SAMUEL C., JR. *The Scouting Expeditions of McCulloch's Texas Rangers; or, the Summer and Fall Campaign of the Army of the United States in Mexico—1846; Including Skirmishes with the Mexicans, and an Accurate Detail of the Storming of Monterrey; also, the Daring Scouts at Buena Vista; Together with Anecdotes, Incidents, Descriptions of Country, and Sketches of the Lives of the Celebrated Partisan Chiefs, Hays, McCulloch, and Walker.* Philadelphia, 1847. (LC)

[ROBB, JOHN S.]. *Streaks of Squatter Life, and Far-West Scenes, a Series of Humorous Sketches Descriptive of Incidents and Character in the Wild West, to Which Are Added Other Miscellaneous Pieces.* Philadelphia, 1847. (LC)

ROBINSON, J. H. *The Life and Adventures of Wm. Harvard Stinchfield, or the Wanderings of a Traveling Merchant.* Portland, Maine, 1851. (LC)

————. *The Lone Star; or, The Texan Bravo, a Tale of the Southwest.* Boston, 1852. (LC)

————. *The Maid of the Ranche; or, the Regulators and Moderators, a Tale of Life on the Texan Frontier.* New York [c1858]. (H)

S. *The Texas Question, Reviewed by an Adopted Citizen, Having Twenty-one Years of Residence in the United States.* New York, 1844. (LC)

SEALSFIELD, CHARLES [POSTL, KARL ANTON]. *The Cabin Book; or, National Characteristics.* Translated from the German by Sarah Powell. New York, 1871. (LC)

[SEALSFIELD, CHARLES]. *Frontier Life, or Tales of the Southwestern Border.* New York, 1859. (LC)

[SEALSFIELD, CHARLES]. *Life in the New World; or Sketches of American Society.* Translated from the German by Gustavus C. Hebbe, L.L.D. and James Mackay, M.A. New York, 1844. Includes *The Cabin Book, or Sketches of Life in Texas.* (LC).

SIMMS, WILLIAM GILMORE. *Confession; or, the Blind Heart, a Domestic Story.* (First Edition, Philadelphia, 1841), New York, 1885. (LC)

Sketches of the Campaign in Northern Mexico, in Eighteen Hundred Forty-six and Seven, by an Officer of the First Regiment of Ohio Volunteers. New York, 1853. (UT)

SMITH, EDWARD. *Account of a Journey Through North-Eastern Texas, Undertaken in 1849, for the Purposes of Emigration.* London, 1849. (UT)

[SMITH, RICHARD PENN]. *Col. Crockett's Exploits and Adventures in Texas: Wherein Is Contained a Full Account of His Journey from Tennessee to the Red River and Natchitoches, and Thence Across Texas to San Antonio; Including His Many Hair-breadth Escapes; Together with a Topographical, Historical, and Political View of Texas.* Philadelphia, 1836. (LC)

SMITH, SOL[OMON FRANKLIN]. *Theatrical Management in the West and South for Thirty Years, Interspersed with Anecdotal Sketches.* New York, 1868. (LC)

STIFF, COL. EDWARD. *The Texan Emigrant: Being a Narration of the Adventures of the Author in Texas, and a Description of the Soil, Climate, Productions, Minerals, Towns, Bays, Harbors, Rivers, Institutions, and Manners and Customs of the Inhabitants of That Country.* Cincinnati, 1840. (UT)

SWEET, ALEXANDER E. and KNOX, J. ARMOY. *Sketches from "Texas Siftings."* New York, 1882. (LC)

TAYLOR, NATHANIEL A. and McDANIELD, H. F. *The Coming Empire; or 2000 Miles in Texas on Horseback.* New York, 1878. (LC)

[THOMPSON, HENRY]. *Texas: Sketches of Character; Moral and Political Condition of the Republic; the Judiciary, &c.* Philadelphia, 1839. (UT)

THORPE, T. B. *Mysteries of the Backwoods; or, Sketches of the Southwest: Including Character, Scenery, and Rural Sports.* Philadelphia, 1846. (LC)

———. *Our Army at Monterey, Being a Correct Account of the Proceedings and Events Which Occurred to the "Army of Occupation" Under the Command of Major General Taylor, from the Time of Leaving Matamoras to the Surrender of Monterey, with a Description of the Three Days' Battle and the Storming of Monterey: the Ceremonies Attending the Surrender: Together with the Particulars of the Capitulation.* Philadelphia, 1847. (LC)

TOMLIN, JOHN. *Tales of the Caddo.* Cincinnati, 1849. (LC)

TROLLOPE, MRS. [FRANCES]. *Domestic Manners of the Americans.* New York, 1832. (UT)

TUCKERMAN, HENRY T. *America and Her Commentators, with a Critical Sketch of Travel in the United States.* New York, 1864. (UT)

VIELE, MRS. *"Following the Drum": A Glimpse of Frontier Life.* New York, 1858. (UT)

[WALTON, WILLIAM]. *Thrilling Incidents of the Wars of the United States: Comprising the Most Striking and Remarkable Events of the Revolution, the French War, the Tripolitan War, the Indian War, the Second War with Great Britain, and the Mexican War.* Philadelphia, 1848. (LC)

WEBBER, CHARLES WILKINS. *The Gold Mines of the Gila, a Sequel to Old Hicks the Guide.* New York, 1849. (LC)

[WEBBER, CHARLES WILKINS]. *Jack Long; or Shot in the Eye: a True Story of Texas Border Life.* New York, 1846. (UT)

WEBBER, CHARLES WILKINS. *Old Hicks the Guide, or, Adventures in the Camanche Country in Search of a Gold Mine.* New York, 1848. (LC)

[WEBBER, CHARLES WILKINS]. *The Prairie Scout, or Agatone the Renegade, a Romance of Border Life.* New York, 1852. (LC)

WEBBER, CHARLES WILKINS. *Tales of the Southern Border.* Philadelphia, 1853. (LC)
———. *Wild Scenes and Wild Hunters of the World.* Philadelphia, 1852. (LC)

WEMYSS, FRANCIS COURTNEY. *Twenty-six Years of the Life of an Actor and Manager: Interspersed with Sketches, Anecdotes and Opinions of the Professional Merits of the Most Celebrated Actors and Actresses of Our Day.* 2 vols. New York, 1847. (LC)

WHITMAN, WALT. *Leaves of Grass.* New York, 1855. (Y)
———. *Leaves of Grass, Selected with Introduction by Christopher Morley.* New York, 1940. (LC)

WORTLEY, LADY EMMELINE STUART. *Travels in the United States, Etc. During 1849 and 1850.* New York, 1851. (UT)

ALMANACS *(primary)*

Ben Hardin's Crockett Almanac, Rows, Sprees, and Scrapes in the West: Life and Manners in the Backwoods: and Terrible Adventures on the Ocean. Baltimore, 1842. (AAS) (LC)

Brother Jonathan's Almanac. Philadelphia, 1847. (LC)

Comic Texas Oldmanick: with Comic Engravings of all the Principal Events of Texas. New York, 1836. (LC)

Crockett's Almanac. Boston, 1848 (LC), New York and Philadelphia, 1848 (AAS)

Crockett Almanac. Boston, 1849. (AAS)

Crockett Almanac. New York, 1856. (AAS)

Crockett Almanac, Containing Adventures, Exploits, Sprees, and Scrapes in the West, and Life and Manners in the Backwoods. Vol. II, no. 1. Nashville, 1839. (AAS)

Crockett Almanac, Containing Adventures, Exploits, Sprees, and Scrapes in the West, and Life and Manners in the Backwoods. Nashville, 1840. (AAS)

Crockett's Almanac, Containing Rows, Sprees, and Scrapes in the West; Life and Manners in the Backwoods. Philadelphia, 1850. (AAS)

Crockett Almanac, Containing Life, Manners, and Adventures in the Backwoods, and Rows, Sprees, and Scrapes on the Western Waters. New York, 1854. (AAS)

Crockett's Almanac, Containing Life, Manners and Adventures in the Back Woods, and Rows, Sprees, and Scrapes on the Western Waters. Philadelphia, New York, and Boston, 1851. (AAS)

Crockett's Almanac; Scenes in River Life, Feats on the Lakes, Manners in the Backwoods, Adventures in Texas &c &c. Philadelphia and Boston, 1846. (LC)

Crockett Comic Almanac. New York, 1839. (LC)

Crockett Comic Almanac. New York, 1842. (LC)

Crockett's Texas Oldmanick, Crockett Goes-Ahead, though Dead. Millions for Texas! But not a Cent for Taxes!!! With Comic Engravings of all the Principal Events of Texas. New York and Philadelphia, 1837. (LC)

Crockett's Yaller Flower Almanac, Go Ahead! Snooks, No Danger Her Going Off! New York, 1836. (AAS)

Davy Crockett's Almanac; Daring Adventures in the Back Woods; Wonderful Scenes in River Life; Manners of Warfare in the West; Feats on the Prairies, in Texas and Oregon. New York, 1847. (LC)

Davy Crockett's Almanac, Life and Manners in the Backwoods; Terrible Battles and Adventures of Border Life. New York, 1844. (AAS)

Davy Crockett's Almanack, of Wild Sports of the West, and Life in the Backwoods; Calculated for all States in the Union. Nashville, 1835. (AAS)

Davy Crockett's Almanack, of Wild Sports in the West, and Life in the Backwoods. Calculated for all the States in the Union. Vol. I, no. 2. Nashville, 1836. (AAS)

Davy Crockett's Almanack, of Wild Sports in the West, Life in the Backwoods, & Sketches of Texas. Vol. I, no. 3. Nashville, 1837. (AAS)

Davy Crockett's Almanack, of Wild Sports in the West, Life in the Backwoods, Sketches of Texas, and Rows on the Mississippi. Nashville, 1838. (LC)

Devil's Comical Texas Oldmanick, The: with Comic Engravings of all the Principal Events of Texas. Philadelphia and New York, 1836. (LC)

Fisher's Comic Almanac. Philadelphia, 1841. (LC)

Gen. Zachary Taylor's Old Rough and Ready Almanac for the Year of Our Lord 1848. Philadelphia, 1848. (NYPL)

Old American Comic Almanac, The, Containing Humorous Designs, Stories and Anecdotes. Boston, 1843. (LC)

Rough and Ready Almanac for 1847. Cincinnati, 1847. (LC)

Rough and Ready Almanac for 1849. Philadelphia, 1849. (NYPL)

Squatter's Almanac, The. New York and Philadelphia, 1845. (LC)

Turner's Comic Almanac. Boston, 1845. (LC)

Turner's Comick Almanack. New York, 1840. (LC)

MAGAZINE ARTICLES (*primary*)

"American Humor," *United States Magazine and Democratic Review*, XVII (September, 1845). (LC)

"Buckeye Celebration, The," *Western Monthly Magazine*, III (June, 1835), 42-50. (LC)

"Captain Marryat and His Diary," *Southern Literary Messenger*, VII (April, 1841), 253-76. (LC)

DURANG, CHARLES. "The Philadelphia Stage from the Year 1749 to the Year 1855. Third Series Embracing the Period Between the Season of 1830-1 and the Demolition of the Chestnut Street Theatre, April, 1855," *Philadelphia Sunday Dispatch*, July 8, 1860 through April 5, 1863. (LC)

"East and the West, The," *United States Magazine and Democratic Review*, XXII (May, 1848), 401-9. (LC)

EMERSON, RALPH WALDO. "The Young American," *Dial*, IV (April, 1844). (UT)

FLINT, TIMOTHY. "Downfall of the Fredonian Republic," *Western Monthly Review*, I (June, 1827), 69-71. (LC)

———. "National Character of the Western People," *Western Monthly Review*, I (July, 1827), 133-39. (LC)

———. "Writers of the Western Country," *Western Monthly Review*, II (June, 1828), 11-21. (LC)

"Kentuckian in New York, The," *Western Monthly Review*, I (June, 1827), 85-88. (LC)

LECLERC, FREDERICK. "Texas and Its Revolution," *Southern Literary Messenger*, VII (May and June, 1841), 398-421. (LC)

"Mission of the Novellettes," *Holden's Dollar Magazine*, I (April, 1848), 217-19. (LC)

"Notes on Texas," *Hesperian: or, Western Monthly Magazine*, I (September, October, November, and December, 1838), II (January, February, March, and April, 1839). (UT)

"Present State of Texas," *Chambers's Edinburgh Journal* (October 7, 1843), 302-3. (UT)

PRIESTLEY, PHILANDER. "Texas," *American Farmer*, XIV (June 29, 1832), 126-27. (LC)

SLY, CHRISTOPHER. "Extracts from a Scrap-book," *Western Monthly Review*, II (July, 1828), 73-78. (LC)

"Texan Mounted Militia" (a picture), *Illustrated London News*, I (1842), 81. (LC)

[WEBBER, CHARLES WILKINS]. "By Charles Winterfield," "Jack Long; or, Lynch-Law and Vengeance," *American Review*, I (February, 1845), 121-36. (LC)

NEWSPAPERS (primary)

In citing the newspapers which aided this study, I shall make no attempt to specify all the issues that helped me. Many simply supplied general background information. Those which gave specific information have been credited accordingly in the footnotes to my text. Except where noted, these papers are all at LC. The issues read are before 1865.

Austin, Texas: *Daily Republican, Daily Texian, Weekly Texian, State Gazette.*

Boston: *Daily Times and Bay State Democrat, Flag of Our Union, Times.*

Brazoria, Texas: *Constitutional Advocate and Texas Public Advertiser.*

Galveston, Texas: *Daily Advertiser, Galvestonian, Daily News, Texas Times.*

Houston, Texas: *Morning Star, National Banner, National Intelligencer, Telegraph and Texas Register, Texian Democrat, Weekly Houstonian, Weekly Times.*

Huntsville, Texas: *Texas Banner.*

London, England: *Theatrical Observer; and Daily Bills of the Play.*

Matagorda, Texas: *Bulletin, Colorado Gazette and Advertiser.*

New Orleans: *Le Courier, Picayune.*

New York: *Brother Jonathan, Daily Globe, Herald, Knickerbocker, Morning Star, New World, Niles Register, Spirit of the Times, Star, Sun, Sunday Dispatch, Sunday Morning News, Weekly Yankee.*

Philadelphia and New York: *Dramatic Mirror and Literary Companion.*

Philadelphia: *Pennsylvanian, Public Ledger and Daily Transcript.*

Portland, Maine: *Daily American.*

San Antonio, Texas: *Western Texan.*

San Augustine, Texas: *Red-Lander.*

San Felipe de Austin, Texas: *Texas Gazette.* (NYPL and UT)

San Luis, Texas: *Advocate.*

Victoria, Texas: *Texian Advocate.*

Washington, Texas: *National Vindicator, Texian and Brazos Farmer.*

PLAYS (primary)

JOHNSTONE, JOHN BEER. *Jack Long, or, the Shot in the Eye.* DeWitt's Acting Plays, No. 100, New York [185-?]. (LC)

ROBINSON, JOHN HOVEY. *The Lone Star: or, the Texan Bravo. A Tale of the Southwest.* Boston, 1852. (LC)

[SIMMS, WILLIAM GILMORE]. "By a Southron," *Michael Bonham: or, the Fall of Bexar. A Tale of Texas.* In Five Parts. Richmond, Virginia, 1852. (LC)

SONGBOOKS (primary)

Crockett's Free and Easy Song Book: A New Collection of the Most Popular Stage Songs, as Given by the Best Vocalists of the Present Day; and also of Favourite Dinner and Parlour Songs. Philadelphia, 1837. (UT)

Crockett's Free and Easy Song Book, Comic, Sentimental, Amatory, Sporting, African, Scotch, Irish, Western and Texian. Philadelphia, 1846. (NYPL)

Rough and Ready Melodist. New York, 1848. (LC)

Rough and Ready Songster: Embellished with Twenty-Five Splendid Engravings, Illustrative of the American Victories in Mexico. New York [1848?]. (UT)

BROADSIDES (*primary*)

"Anti-Texas Meeting at Faneuil Hall." Boston, January 24, 1838. (LC)

"The Meeting in Faneuil Hall; to Protest Against the Annexation of Texas." Boston, 1838. (LC)

"Petition to Congress and Petition to Various Legislatures Opposing Annexation of Texas." [Boston?, 1838?] (LC)

"Statistics of the United States and Texas." Auburn, New York. (LC)

BOOKS (*secondary*)

BANCROFT, HUBERT HOWE. *History of the North Mexican States and Texas.* San Francisco, 1889.

BARKER, EUGENE C. *The Life of Stephen F. Austin: Founder of Texas, 1793-1836: A Chapter in the Westward Movement of the Anglo-American People.* Nashville, Tennessee, 1925.

BLAIR, WALTER. *Horse Sense in American Humor: From Benjamin Franklin to Ogden Nash.* Chicago, 1942.

———. *Native American Humor 1800-1900.* New York, 1937.

BOYNTON, HENRY WALCOTT. *Annals of American Bookselling 1638-1850.* New York, 1932.

BRADSHER, EARL L. *Mathew Carey, Editor, Author and Publisher: A Study in American Literary Development.* New York, 1912.

BRIGHAM, CLARENCE. *An Account of American Almanacs and Their Value for Historical Study.* Worcester, Massachusetts, 1925.

BROGAN, D. W. *The American Character.* New York, 1944.

BROWN, T[HOMAS] ALLSTON. *A History of the New York Stage: From the First Performance in 1732 to 1901.* 3 vols. New York, 1903.

CURTI, MERLE. *The Growth of American Thought.* New York, 1943.

DE VOTO, BERNARD. *Mark Twain's America.* New York, 1932.

DORSON, RICHARD M. *Davy Crockett: American Comic Legend.* New York, 1939.

FAUST, ALBERT B. *Charles Sealsfield: Materials for a Biography; a Study of His Style; His Influence upon American Literature.* Baltimore, 1892.

GAFFORD, LUCILE. *A History of the St. Charles Theatre in New Orleans 1835-1843.* Chicago, 1932.

GABRIEL, RALPH HENRY. *The Course of American Democratic Thought: An Intellectual History Since 1815.* New York, 1940.

HOGAN, WILLIAM RANSOM. *The Texas Republic: a Social and Economic History.* Norman, Oklahoma, 1946.

HOOLE, WILLIAM STANLEY. *Sam Slick in Texas.* San Antonio, Texas, 1945.

JAMES, MARQUIS. *The Raven: a Biography of Sam Houston.* Indianapolis, 1929.

LEHMANN-HAUPT, HELLMUT. *The Book in America: a History of the Making, the Selling, and the Collecting of Books in the United States.* New York, 1939.

LYNCH, JAMES D. *The Bench and Bar of Texas*. St. Louis, 1885.

MASTERSON, JAMES R. *Tall Tales of Arkansaw*. Boston, 1943.

McCULLOUGH, BRUCE W. *The Life and Writings of Richard Penn Smith: with a Reprint of His Play, "The Deformed."* Menasha, Wisconsin, 1917.

MEINE, FRANKLIN J. *Tall Tales of the Southwest: an Anthology of Southern and Southwestern Humor, 1830-1860*. New York, 1930.

MUDD, ALOYSIUS I. "The Theatres of Washington from 1835 to 1850," *Columbia Historical Society Records*, VI, 1903. (LC)

MURRELL, WILLIAM. *A History of American Graphic Humor*. 2 vols. New York, 1933.

NEVINS, ALLAN. *American Social History as Recorded by British Travellers*. New York, 1924.

ODELL, GEORGE C. D. *Annals of the NewYork Stage*. 14 vols. NewYork, 1927-49.

ODUM, HOWARD W. and MOORE, HARRY E. *American Regionalism, a Cultural-Historical Approach to National Integration*. New York, 1938.

ORIANS, GEORGE HARRISON. *The Influence of Walter Scott upon America and American Literature Before 1860*. Urbana, Illinois, 1929.

PARRINGTON, V. L. *Main Currents in American Thought*. 3 vols. New York, 1927.

PEARSON, EDMUND LESTER. *Dime Novels; or, Following an Old Trail in Popular Literature*. Boston, 1929.

QUINN, ARTHUR HOBSON. *A History of the American Drama from the Beginning to the Civil War*. New York, 1923.

ROURKE, CONSTANCE. *American Humor; a Study of the National Character*. New York, 1931.

———. *Davy Crockett*. New York, 1934.

———. *The Roots of American Culture*. New York, 1942.

SEYBOLT, PAUL S. *The First Editions of Henry William Herbert "Frank Forester" 1807-1858*. Boston, 1932.

SMITH, HENRY NASH. *Virgin Land: the American West as Symbol and Myth*. Cambridge, Massachusetts, 1950.

SMITH, JUSTIN HARVEY. *The Annexation of Texas*. Cor. ed. New York, 1941.

———. *The War with Mexico*. New York, 1919.

SMITHER, NELLE. *A History of the English Theatre at New Orleans 1806-1842*. Philadelphia, 1944.

TOMPKINS, EUGENE. *The History of the Boston Theatre 1854-1901*. Boston, 1908.

TURNER, FREDERICK JACKSON. *The Frontier in American History*. New York, 1921.

———. *The Significance of Sections in American History*. New York, 1932.

WEBB, WALTER PRESCOTT. *The Great Plains*. New York, 1931.

———. *The Texas Rangers: a Century of Frontier Defense*. Boston, 1935.

WHITE, LUKE, JR. *Henry William Herbert and the American Publishing Scene 1831-1858*. Newark, New Jersey, 1943.

WILSON, ARTHUR HERMAN. *A History of the Philadelphia Theatre, 1835-1855*. Philadelphia, 1935.

WYMAN, MARY ALICE. *Two American Pioneers: Seba Smith and Elizabeth Oakes Smith*. New York, 1927.

MAGAZINE ARTICLES *(secondary)*

BARKER, E. C. "Notes on Early Texas Newspapers—1819-1836," *Southwestern Historical Quarterly,* XXI (July, 1917), 127-44.

"Biography of Richard Penn Smith," *Burton's Gentleman's Magazine,* V (September, 1839). (LC)

BLAIR, WALTER. "Six Davy Crocketts," *Southwest Review,* XXV (July, 1940), 443-62.

BOATRIGHT, MODY C. "Frontier Humor; Despairing or Buoyant?" *Southwest Review,* XXVII (Spring, 1942), 320-35.

CLARK, THOMAS D. "Manners and Humors of the American Frontier," *Missouri Historical Review,* XXXV (October, 1940), 3-24.

DEWEY, JOHN. "Americanism and Localism," *Dial,* LXVIII (June, 1920), 684-88.

DORSON, RICHARD M. "The Yankee on the Stage," *New England Quarterly,* XIII (September, 1940), 467-93.

DYKES, J. C. "Dime Novel Texas; or, the Sub-literature of the Lone Star State," *Southwestern Historical Quarterly,* XLIX (January, 1946), 327-40.

HALE, EDWARD E. "The Romantic Landscape of the Far West," *Faculty Papers of Union College, Union College Bulletin,* XXIII, No. 2 (January, 1930), 5-17. (LC)

HOGAN, WILLIAM R. "The Theater in the Republic of Texas," *Southwest Review,* XIX (July, 1934), 374-401.

JORDAN, PHILLIP D. "Humor of the Backwoods, 1820-1840," *Mississippi Valley Historical Review,* XXV (June, 1942), 25-38.

MACMINN, G. R. " 'The Gen'lman from Pike' in Early California," *American Literature,* VIII (May, 1936), 160-69.

ROLLER, JOHN E. "Capt. John Sowers Brooks," *Texas Historical Association Quarterly,* IX (January, 1906), 157-209.

ROURKE, CONSTANCE. "Davy Crockett: Forgotten Facts and Legends," *Southwest Review,* XIX (January, 1934), 149-61.

———. "Examining the Roots of American Humor," *American Scholar,* IV (Spring, 1935).

———. "The Significance of Sections," *New Republic* (September 20, 1933), 148-51.

SCHLESINGER, ARTHUR M. "What Then Is the American, This New Man?" *American Historical Review,* XLVIII (January, 1943), 225-44.

INDEX

Typography by CARL HERTZOG *El Paso, Texas*

Presswork: Guynes Printing Company, *El Paso*

Binding: H. V. Chapman & Sons, *Abilene*

Text Type: Caledonia

Headings: Bulmer Italic

Title: Weiss Initials

Paper: Maxwell Vellum Offset